The Impact of Illegal Immigration on the Wages and Employment Opportunities of Black Workers

A Briefing Before
The United States Commission on Civil Rights
Held in Washington, DC

Briefing Report

Letter of Transmittal

The President
The President of the Senate
The Speaker of the House

Sirs and Madam:

The United States Commission on Civil Rights (Commission) is pleased to transmit this report, *The Impact of Illegal Immigration on the Wages and Employment Opportunities of Black Workers*. A panel of experts briefed members of the Commission on April 4, 2008 regarding the evidence for economic loss and job opportunity costs to black workers attributable to illegal immigration. The panelists also described non-economic factors contributing to the depression of black wages and employment rates. Based on that discussion, the Commission developed the findings and recommendation that are included in this report.

Among its findings, the Commission notes that the illegal workers are estimated to account for as much as one-third of total immigrants in the United States, and that illegal immigration has tended to increase the supply of low-skilled, low-wage labor available. The Commission found also that about six in 10 adult black males have a high school diploma or less, and are disproportionately employed in the low-skilled labor market in likely competition with immigrants. Evidence for negative effects of such competition ranged from modest to significant, according to the experts who testified, but even those experts who viewed the effects as modest overall found significant effects in occupations such as meatpacking and construction.

The Commission views this topic as complex, and therefore makes no specific recommendations at this time. The Commission recommends generally, however, that the Bureau of Labor Statistics and other appropriate governmental agencies collect data concerning the presence of illegal workers in the U.S. workforce and on the employment and wage rate effects of such workers on low-skilled and low-wage workers of all races. The Commission believes that such data should be made available to the public.

Part A, which consists of the body of this report, was approved on January 15, 2010 by Chairman Reynolds and Commissioners Kirsanow, Heriot, and Taylor. Vice Chair Thernstrom and Commissioners Gaziano and Melendez abstained. Commissioner Yaki voted against. Vote tallies for each of the Commission's findings and recommendation, which make up Part B of the report, are noted therein.

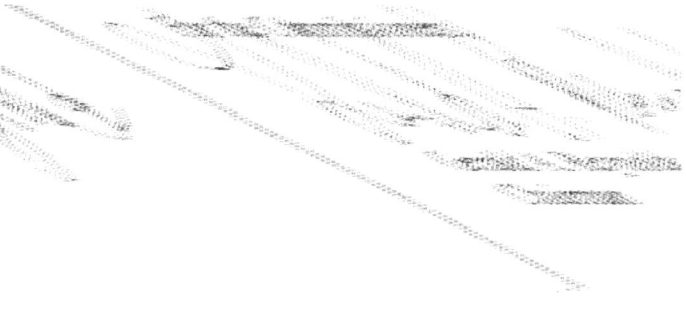

Table of Contents

Executive Summary

In the midst of public debate over immigration reform, the U.S. Commission on Civil Rights voted to examine the possible effects of illegal immigration on particularly vulnerable segments of the U.S. working population, specifically low-skill black workers.[1] Since the April 4, 2008 briefing, the severe economic downturn has affected workers in general, and--if unemployment rates are any indication--has had an even more severe impact on low-skill workers.[2]

To help air important aspects of the debate, the Commission invited experts who have published and spoken on this issue to weigh the relative effects of factors that influence black low-skill workers' wages, job gains or losses and report their conclusions to the Commission. The speakers discussed factors that included the economic costs to this particular group,[3] fiscal costs to taxpayers of social services for low-skill workers, competing skill levels of affected workers, the economic gains to the U.S. economy as a whole from flexible, low-cost labor,[4] and what constitutes a fair comparison between legal and illegal workers and their job opportunities.[5]

The Commission selected balanced panels that included Harry Holzer, professor of public policy at Georgetown University; Gordon H. Hanson, professor of economics at the University of California, San Diego; Julie Hotchkiss, research economist and policy advisor at the Federal Reserve Bank of Atlanta; Vernon Briggs, professor emeritus of labor economics at Cornell University; Gerald Jaynes, professor of economics and African American Studies at Yale University; Richard Nadler, president of Americas Majority Foundation; Carol Swain, professor of political science and law at Vanderbilt University; and Steven Camarota, director of research at the Center for Immigration Studies in Washington, DC.

---

[1] *See, e.g.*, Lori Montgomery, "Immigration Lifts Wages, Report Says, White House Asserts Only Least-Skilled Native Workers Are Hurt," Washington Post, June 21, 2007, at D3.; Charles Herman, "Illegals: Will They Be Taking Jobs Away From U.S. Citizens?" ABC News Business Unit, May 18, 2007, http://abcnews.go.com/Business/IndustryInfo/story?id=3189288&page=1; "Illegal Aliens Depress Wages for Some in US," New York Times, March 20, 1988, at section 1, p. 25.

[2] The Bureau of Labor Statistics notes that as of November 2008, unemployment rates for individuals over the age of 25 with less than a high school diploma was 15.0%, 5 percent more than the national unemployment average of 10 percent for the same time period.

[3] *See, e.g.*, Vernon M. Briggs, Jr., "The Economic Well-Being of Black Americans: The Overarching Influence of U.S. Immigration Policies," The Review of Black Political Economy, 15-42 (2003).

[4] *See, e.g.*, Gordon H. Hanson, "The Economic Logic of Illegal Immigration," Council on Foreign Relations, CSR No. 26, April 2007, http://www.cfr.org/content/publications/attachments/ImmigrationCSR26.pdf. (accessed August 31, 2009).

[5] *See, e.g.*, George J. Borjas, Jeffrey Grogger, and Gordon H. Hanson, "Imperfect Substitution Between Immigrants and Natives: A Reappraisal," March, 2008, http://irps.ucsd.edu/assets/022/8778.pdf (accessed August 31, 2009); *but see* Gianmarco Ottaviano and Giovanni Peri, "The Effects of Immigration on U.S. Wages and Rents: A General Equilibrium Approach," September 26, 2007, http://www.econ.ucdavis.edu/faculty/gperi/Papers/Perott_city_Sept_2007.pdf (accessed September 9, 2009).

Although available data did not distinguish precisely between legal and illegal immigration in their effects on wages and employment of black workers, most panelists agreed that illegal immigration appears to have had at least some negative effects on the wages and employment of workers in the low-skill labor market. The panelists disagreed as to the magnitude of that effect, which ranged from very small to substantial. Three of the panelists who were economists argued that immigration, both legal and illegal, has economically benefited the United States on a national basis in the form of lower prices to consumers and increased economic investment in the country.[6] One presented employment statistics only for the State of Georgia that she asserted could be generalized to a nationwide inquiry, but did not express an opinion as to the magnitude of the national effects.[7] Another panelist spoke to the specific negative effects of illegal immigration on the population at risk, black male workers.[8]

The panelists addressed the following issues in response to Commissioners' questions:

- The consensus by panelists that there is a negative effect on wages of low-skill black workers and the range of the negative effects;

- The importance of other factors contributing to low-skill black unemployment;

- Possible discrimination resulting from the use of ethnic networks;

- Benefits and costs to the U.S. economy from illegal immigration;

- Policy recommendations from panelists, including strict enforcement of existing immigration laws;

- Effect of capital flows, including those across and within national borders, that decrease the negative effects of immigration;

- Tradeoffs to employers between increasing their capital investment versus hiring more low-wage workers;

- The potential disruption to the economy and to low-wage workers and communities of abrupt economic changes resulting from enforcing immigration laws strictly;

- The sharp differences between the employment opportunities of low-skill black men and low-skill black women;

- The ethical and civil rights implications of using immigration to drive down low-skill wages.

---

[6] Dr. Hanson, Dr. Jaynes, and Dr. Holzer.

[7] Dr. Hotchkiss.

[8] Dr. Swain.

Findings and Recommendation

Findings

1. There has been a significant rise in U.S. immigration, both legal and illegal, over the past four decades. Experts at our briefing testified that immigrant workers now make up approximately one-seventh of the American workforce, and they estimated that illegal workers account for one-third of the total immigrants now in the U.S. [Approved (4-1): Chairman Reynolds and Commissioners Gaziano, Heriot and Kirsanow voted in favor; Commissioner Yaki voted against; Commissioner Taylor did not vote.]

2. Illegal immigration to the United States in recent decades has tended to increase the supply of low-skilled, low-wage labor available in the U.S. labor market. [Approved (5-1): Chairman Reynolds and Commissioners Gaziano, Heriot, Kirsanow, and Taylor voted in favor; Commissioner Yaki voted against.]

3. About six in 10 adult black males have a high school diploma or less, and black men are disproportionately employed in the low-skilled labor market, where they are more likely to be in labor competition with immigrants. [Approved (4-1): Chairman Reynolds and Commissioners Heriot, Kirsanow and Taylor voted in favor; Commissioner Yaki voted against; Commissioner Gaziano abstained.]

4. The average worker with a high school degree or less earns less today, adjusted for inflation, than someone with a similar education earned thirty-five years ago. [Approved (5-1): Chairman Reynolds and Commissioners Gaziano, Heriot, Kirsanow, and Taylor voted in favor; Commissioner Yaki voted against.]

5. Illegal immigration to the United States in recent decades has tended to depress both wages and employment rates for low-skilled American citizens, a disproportionate number of whom are black men. Expert economic opinions concerning the negative effects range from modest to significant. Those panelists that found modest effects overall nonetheless found significant effects in industry sectors such as meatpacking and construction. [Approved (5-1): Chairman Reynolds and Commissioners Gaziano, Heriot, Kirsanow, and Taylor voted in favor; Commissioner Yaki voted against.]

6. To be sure, factors other than illegal immigration contribute to black unemployment. The problem cannot be solved without solving the problems of the high school dropout rate, high rates of family instability, and low job-retention rates. Moreover, halting illegal immigration is not a panacea even for the problem of depressed wage rates for low-skilled jobs. If upward pressure is brought to bear on low-skilled wages, increasing globalization of the economy may result in some of these jobs simply being exported to other countries. Still, the effect of illegal immigration on the wages of low-skilled workers, who are disproportionately minority members, is a piece of the puzzle that must be considered by policymakers in formulating sound immigration policy. [Approved (5-1): Chairman Reynolds and Commissioners Gaziano, Heriot, Kirsanow, and Taylor voted in favor; Commissioner Yaki voted against.]

7. Data collection and analysis of the effects of illegal immigration are necessary to develop sound public policy. Much of the data on this question is currently limited by the fact that it does not distinguish clearly between legal and illegal immigration. [Approved (5-1: Chairman Reynolds and Commissioners Gaziano, Heriot, Kirsanow, and Taylor voted in favor; Commissioner Yaki voted against.]

Recommendation

The issue of illegal immigration is so complex that it would not be appropriate for us to make specific recommendations at this time. However, the Commission does recommend that the Bureau of Labor Statistics and other appropriate governmental agencies should collect data concerning the presence of illegal workers in the U.S. workforce and compile data on the employment and wage rate effects of such workers on low-skilled and low-wage workers of all races, making such data available to the public. [Approved (5-1): Chairman Reynolds and Commissioners Gaziano, Heriot, Kirsanow, and Taylor voted in favor; Commissioner Yaki voted against.]

Summary of Proceedings

Panel One

Gordon Hanson

Professor Hanson[9] began his remarks by noting the dramatic rise in U.S. immigration, which rose from 5 percent in the 1970s to 12 percent by 2006. According to Dr. Hanson, immigrant workers make up one-seventh of the American workforce, and illegal workers account for one-third of the total immigrants now in the U.S. Dr. Hanson stated that around 60 percent of illegal immigrants have less than a high school education and compete for low-skilled jobs with native workers. He observed that economic theory would predict downward wage pressure as the result of the increase in the supply of workers in the U.S. economy. He noted the disagreement among economists, however, as to whether the data allows such a conclusion, indicating that studies on wage trends in different local labor markets often find small effects, and studies that look at wages on a national basis find larger effects. He stated that the strongest adverse impacts would be felt by workers competing for jobs with immigrants directly, that is, by low-skilled native workers.

His co-authored study[10] based on these data found that the employment rate of black high school dropouts fell from 72 percent in 1960 to 42 percent in 2000, compared to an 83 to 64 percent decline among white high school dropouts. In addition, the number of black men in correctional institutions rapidly increased during a shorter period (1980–2000), going from 1.4 percent of black high school dropouts to 21 percent.

Dr. Hanson noted that, surprisingly, there is little research on the connection between immigration and the employment and incarceration of black men. He questioned whether diminished wages resulting from immigration have encouraged some black men to leave the labor force and turn to crime.

To find the specific effects of immigration on black low-wage workers, Professor Hanson and his coauthors examined U.S. census data from 1960 to 2000 and found a strong correlation between immigration, wages, employment rates, and incarceration rates for

---

[9] Gordon Hanson, testimony, pp. 8–16. Briefing transcript of record before the U.S. Commission on Civil Rights, Impact of Illegal Immigration on the Wages & Employment of Black Workers, Washington, DC, Apr. 4, 2008, (Hereinafter cited as "Briefing Transcript").

[10] Borjas, Grogger and Hanson, "Immigration and African-American Employment Opportunities: The Response of Wages, Employment and Incarceration to Labor Supply Shocks," 2006, NBER Working Paper 12518, http://ksghome harvard.edu/~GBorjas/Papers/Borjas,%20Grogger,%20Hanson,%202006.pdf; *see also* Borjas, Grogger and Hanson, "Immigration and the Economic Status of African-American Men," January, 2009, http://irps.ucsd.edu/assets/027/9473.pdf, cf. Footnote 11; for a related inquiry concerning the United Kingdom, *see also* "The Economic Impact of Immigration," House of Lords Economic Affairs Committee, HL Paper 82-I, 2008, http://www.publications.parliament.uk/pa/ld200708/ldselect/ldeconaf/82/82.pdf (all accessed Apr. 1, 2009)

blacks. He did not address the effects of illegal immigration separately. Dr. Hanson's coauthored research suggested that a 10 percent immigrant-induced increase in the labor supply is associated with a 4 percent decrease in black wages, a 3.5 percent decrease in the black employment rate, and a 0.8 percent increase in the black incarceration rate.[11] This correlation held true in both national and state-level data, according to Hanson. The same data source showed that the effect of immigration on white men also produced a 4.1 percent decrease in wages, but had much less effect on employment and incarceration rates. Thus, wages went down for the skill group generally, but black men lost proportionally more jobs and disproportionally increased in incarceration rates.

Dr. Hanson stated that the economic changes created by the large immigrant inflow from 1980 to 2000 (half of which he attributes to illegal immigration) resulted in a labor supply shock that increased the number of workers in the U.S. by 10 percent, with an increase in the number of high school dropouts in the population by over 20 percent. These adjustments account for about 40 percent of the overall 18 percent decline in black employment rates and 10 of the 20 percentage point increase in the incarceration rate of black high school dropouts over the same period. Dr. Hanson noted that this influx reduced the employment rate of low-skill black men by eight percentage points. Dr. Hanson emphasized that although immigration played an important role in generating these trends, much of the decline in employment and increase in jail time would have occurred with a far smaller immigrant influx, and remains unexplained. He recommended that it not be restricted. In his opinion, the inflow of foreign workers accompanies more productive use of resources such as technology, plants, and equipment, and has brought overall benefits to the U.S. economy; therefore, he recommended instead that the country find ways to help those who have been hurt by immigration.

Gerald Jaynes

Professor Jaynes[12] began his remarks by stating that his views on this topic had changed on the basis of his research on immigration and its effects on race and ethnic relations. He contrasted his initial view that immigration had negative effects on the jobs and wages of blacks with his present view that negative effects are mostly absent or modest at worst, for a small segment of the lowest skilled workers. His thinking changed, he said, due to a large-scale statistical analysis of the U.S. labor market he conducted with University of Wisconsin social demographer Franklin Wilson, which was published in 2000. Among other variables, their study looked at race, ethnicity, gender, and blue-collar versus white-collar workers. Dr.

---

[11] A later paper by Hanson and his colleagues, published in January 2009, only slightly modified these original findings, noting that "a 10 percent immigrant-induced increase in the supply side of a particular skill group is associated with a reduction in the black wage of 2.5 percent, a reduction in the black employment rate of 5.9 percentage points, and an increase in the black institutionalization rate of 1.3 percentage points." See Borjas, Grogger and Hanson, *Immigration and the Economic Status of African-American Men* (Jan. 2009), *at* http://irps.ucsd.edu/assets/027/9473.pdf.

[12] Briefing Transcript, pp. 17–23. *See also*, Gerald Jaynes, Immigration and Race: New Challenges for American Democracy, Yale Univ. Press, 2000; "Economic Effects of Contemporary Immigration," Gerald Jaynes, Testimony presented to the Subcommittee on Immigration, U.S. House of Representatives, Committee on the Judiciary, 110th Congress, May 3, 2007.

Jaynes said he was surprised to discover that employment effects were negligible and wage effects only modestly negative for the least-skilled blacks.

Dr. Jaynes' written testimony recognized that the surge in immigration over the past thirty-five years occurred simultaneously with a large drop in the inflation-adjusted wages of less-educated American workers.[13] Between 1969 and 1984 (measuring in 1984 constant dollars), black male high school graduates' mean weekly wages fell 22 percent from $357 to $278 per week, and for black male dropouts, 32 percent, from $312 to $213. By 1985, the average weekly salary of a black male high school graduate aged 20-24 was $165 per week; for black male dropouts the same age, it was $146 per week. Black male high school dropouts also experienced precipitous increases in unemployment over the same period. Black high-school dropouts had an unemployment rate of 45 percent by the mid-1980s, whereas in 1970, dropouts had an employment rate of 85 percent. But he cautioned that a host of socioeconomic changes provide an alternative explanation for the deteriorating economic circumstances of low-skilled black workers.

Similarly, in his briefing testimony, Dr. Jaynes acknowledged that since his study was published, other economic studies had found negative effects, but he referred to the difficulty of controlling for the increases in competition and international trade, declines in unionization and in blue-collar employment, changes in discrimination that more negatively affect low-skill black workers, and anti-social trends such as lower marital rates. He pointed out that the impact of illegal immigration was difficult to quantify because the data were not precise as to illegal immigrants.[14] As a result of his skepticism of the available data, Dr. Jaynes stated that he would not make recommendations for policy changes relating to the negative effects on the least-skilled black workers.[15]

Vernon Briggs, Jr.

In both his written and oral testimony, Professor Briggs[16] stated that no issue has negatively "affected the economic well-being of African Americans more" than immigration[17]. His view is that blacks have been both victims of involuntary immigration themselves (through slavery) and unintentional, but significant victims of job losses and lowered wages as a result of the mass, low-skilled immigration that has occurred since 1965. Dr. Briggs viewed such losses as a denial of basic civil rights and economic opportunity.[18]

---

[13] In particular, the earnings of full-time high school graduate men fell significantly compared to the earnings of male college graduates of the same age. Jaynes Written Statement, p. 29 of this briefing report.

[14] *But see* Dr. Jaynes's submitted written statement, in which he notes that in some job markets, immigrants exert significant influence on natives' job prospects, showing a significant drop in meatpacking, where undocumented workers composed 25 percent of the workforce in Iowa and Nebraska, and in the poultry industry in the South. Latino immigrants constitute about three-quarters of the poultry workers in Arkansas, for example.

[15] Briefing Transcript, p. 22.

[16] Id. at 23-31.

[17] Id. at 23.

[18] "[W]ith the accidental revival of mass immigration in the years since 1965 that has continued to this day, immigration has served largely to marginalize the imperative to address squarely and affirmatively the legacy of the denial of equal opportunity that had resulted from the previous centuries of slavery and segregation which

Dr. Briggs stated that about 12 million illegal immigrants are currently in the U.S. labor market, which represents about 30 percent of the total foreign-born population in the United States. He added that there have been seven amnesties since 1986, and that in his view, further legalization of such immigrants with family reunification would be economically devastating to low-wage workers of all races and black workers in particular.

Dr. Briggs emphasized that the distinguishing characteristic of the illegal immigrant population is that 81 percent of them are probably in the low-skill sector of the job market; about 57 percent of them are without a high school diploma, and 24 percent have only a high school diploma. Since they often come from poor countries, he said, the quality of their education is likely poor, and they frequently lack English language skills. According to Dr. Briggs, the competition they pose for native youth and 43 million low-skilled U.S. workers causes the low-skilled labor market to suffer the highest unemployment levels of any measured segment. He further noted that the low skilled labor market is most vulnerable to economic hardship. During an economic downturn, higher skilled workers back up into the low skilled labor market, producing even more competition for low-skilled jobs.

Dr. Briggs noted that blacks account for approximately 10 percent of the total low-skilled workforce that numbers about 50 million, but have the highest unemployment rates of any of the four racial or ethnic groups in the data; in February 2008 this rate was 12.8 percent. Black youths also have the highest unemployment rates—in February 2008, it was 31.7 percent, which does not count those discouraged from seeking work, or those who were incarcerated.

Dr. Briggs stated that both black Americans and illegal immigrants are disproportionately concentrated in many central cities of large metropolitan areas where job competition between them is likely to be extensive. In non-metropolitan areas, blacks are found in large numbers only in the rural Southeast—a legacy, he said, of the area's history of slavery—but in recent decades, they have been joined in that labor market by the foreign-born who have grown to be a significant population segment in these rural areas.[19]

He noted that to an immigrant worker, the low wages offered in the U.S. are still higher than in his home country, and thus relatively acceptable, often regardless of the conditions that accompany it.[20] That employers take advantage of this comparison by preferring illegal workers reflects pragmatism by employers, not necessarily bad intent, according to Dr. Briggs. He stated that this occurs because the federal government has not enforced its labor and immigration laws in such workplaces, leaving employers who wish to follow the law at a competitive disadvantage to those who find it more profitable to break it.

---

the civil rights movement and legislation of the 1960s sought to redress." Briggs Written Testimony at p. 36 of this briefing report.

[19] In his briefing testimony, Briggs noted that 26 percent of the nation's foreign-born population now resides in the rural Southeast. Briefing Transcript, p. 29.

[20] For example, illegal immigrants are more likely to take lower wages and work under harsh or dangerous conditions and less likely to complain about sub-minimum wage pay or denial of overtime pay because of the vulnerability imposed by their illegal status. *See* Briggs Written Testimony at p. 39 of this briefing report.

Dr. Briggs also stated that the inflow of immigrants has resulted in low-skilled wages not rising over time.[21] He viewed the reduction of both wages and jobs as a massive violation of the civil rights of all low-skilled workers, and of black workers in particular. He recommended, therefore, that the federal government should adhere to the findings of the U.S. Commission on Immigration Reform, chaired by the late Congresswoman Barbara Jordan (D-TX): "People who should get in, do get in; people who should not get in, are kept out; and people who are judged deportable, are required to leave."[22]

Harry Holzer

Professor Holzer[23] made four major points in his remarks to the Commission. The first was his assertion that most statistical evidence suggests that immigration over the past few decades has had a modest negative effect on the employment outcomes of blacks, especially those without high school diplomas. Dr. Holzer's review of economic studies indicated that work by Borjas, Grogger, and Hanson showed the greatest negative effects on wages and employment of black male high school dropouts. He cautioned, however, that this result was likely overstated, since it was based on significant statistical assumptions and limited also by its short-run assessment of the effect of immigration, which did not take into account capital inflows (meaning investments) that likely mitigated such impacts on black workers. Dr. Holzer added that recent scholarly papers using data across metropolitan areas had found effects ranging from very modest for black men to somewhat larger where black and white teens were studied, but that these effects lessened as they aged into their twenties.

Dr. Holzer's next point was that other evidence, including that by ethnographers, indicates that employers filling low-wage jobs that require little reading/writing or communication, clearly prefer immigrants to native-born blacks, and encourage informal networks through which immigrants gain better access to these jobs. Dr. Holzer's review found that employers prefer immigrants because of a perceived superior work ethic and tolerance for low wages, and use ethnic networks to recruit. He suggested that this might reflect discrimination, although it might also merely reflect real differences, on average, in attitudes and behaviors of workers from different racial and ethnic groups.[24]

His third point was that the evidence does not allow economists to distinguish the effects of legal versus illegal immigration on black workers. Dr. Holzer stated that many black men would likely take residential construction or transportation jobs but doubted whether they would be drawn by the wages offered in agricultural or service jobs, even if the absence of immigrant wages led to an increase in such wages. He said the evidence does not allow clear

---

[21] *See* Vernon Briggs, "U.S. Immigration Policy and the Plight of Unskilled Workers," 1999, http://digitalcommons.ilr.cornell.edu/cgi/viewcontent.cgi?article=1103&context=cahrswp (accessed September 9, 2009).

[22] Briefing Transcript, p. 31 (citing testimony of former U.S. Representative Barbara Jordan (D-TX), Chair, U.S. Commission on Immigration Reform, U.S. House of Representatives, Committee on the Judiciary Subcommittee on Immigration and Claims, Feb. 24, 1995, http://www.utexas.edu/lbj/uscir/022495.html (accessed Oct. 29, 2008)).

[23] Briefing Transcript, pp. 31–38.

[24] Harry Holzer, "The Labor Market and Young Black Men," September, 2007, http://www.urban.org/UploadedPDF/1001111_moynihan_perspective.pdf (accessed September 9, 2009).

distinctions regarding the impact of legal versus illegal immigration on native-born black workers.

Fourth, Dr. Holzer concluded from the modest negative impact of immigration that other factors are much more responsible for the negative trends in employment of black men and their rising incarceration rates, and, therefore, that other policies besides immigration reform might be needed to change these trends. Dr. Holzer suggested that immigration should have similarly affected black women, yet the employment rates of low-income black women improved dramatically during the 1990s because of welfare reform and the expansion of programs such as the Earned Income Tax Credit and child support subsidies.

Dr. Holzer enumerated the forces he believed were more responsible than immigration for the decline in jobs and wages for low-skilled black men and the increase in incarceration rates.[25] These included the decline of well-paying jobs available to less-educated males in general, especially outside the service sector; rising returns to illegal drug trade in the 1980s; growing numbers of blacks in single-parent families in poor neighborhoods; changes in attitudes and behavioral norms related to schooling, marriage and employment; increases in jail sentence time for convictions involving the drug trade; and increased enforcement of child support orders resulting in default judgments.

Dr. Holzer suggested remedies that did not require changes in immigration law, since he said that such changes would be unlikely to produce improved outcomes for low-skilled black workers. These proposed remedies included 1) policies improving educational outcomes throughout all school grades, 2) enhancing youth development opportunities and mentoring for adolescents in black communities, 3) improving early work experience and training with high-quality education, 4) reducing incarceration rates without increasing crime and reducing barriers to work by ex-offenders, 5) extending the Earned Income Tax Credit to childless adults, including non-custodial fathers, and 6) reforming child support regulations to encourage non-custodial fathers to seek and find work.

Discussion

Vice Chair Thernstrom began by asking the first panel, all of whom were labor economists, to comment on each others' remarks in order to clarify the points of agreement and disagreement among those using similar data sets and with similar academic training. Commissioner Kirsanow observed that there appeared to be a consensus that illegal immigration had an impact on wages and that most of the economists viewed it as small, with the exception of Dr. Briggs, who found it egregious.

Dr. Briggs objected to viewing this issue purely in terms of numbers because of what he believed were limitations of the data sets used by econometricians. He specifically criticized the practice of lumping all foreign-born persons together into one category and drawing economic inferences from that grouping as an untenable concept. He stated that some

---

[25] *See also*, "Economic Impacts of Immigration," Holzer, H., Testimony to the Committee on Education and the Workforce, U.S. House of Representatives, Nov. 16, 2005, http://www.urban.org/UploadedPDF/900908_Holzer_111605.pdf (accessed September 9, 2009).

workers in the data sets were naturalized citizens, permanent resident aliens, or non-immigrant workers and others were illegal immigrants, but there was no distinction made between them. He objected strongly on civil rights grounds to permitting competition from illegal sources to depress the wages and job numbers of what he believed are the most vulnerable citizens in our society. He pointed to the depressed wages caused by the desperation of illegal workers for any job and the unfair displacement their sheer numbers (12 to 14 million) are having on the legal low-skill labor force.[26]

Although recognizing the various studies' limitations, Dr. Holzer defended the quality of the data, citing a long tradition of many good empirical comparisons, such as Dr. Hanson's, that looked across metropolitan areas or states, and at aggregated views over time.[27] Dr. Holzer stated that economists' comparisons across geographic areas may understate the effects somewhat, and the comparisons over time perhaps overstate the effects somewhat, but most economists have arrived at a consensus that the effects are modest. He added that the forces affecting wages and employment are much more complicated than Dr. Briggs indicated, and include immigrants as consumers who affect demand for products and services as well as supply. He suggested that immigrants likely generate more capital flowing into the country, more efficiency in the use of capital, and higher economic growth, which offset some of the negative effects on low-skilled black workers. In addition, where there is a lot of low-wage labor available, employers will switch production to more labor-intensive methods, whereas employers without such labor availability will choose more capital-intensive methods rather than raise wages. Finally, he stated that workers sort themselves into different kinds of jobs rather than compete for the same jobs.[28]

Dr. Briggs interjected that Dr. Holzer was referring to all immigration, whereas he (Dr. Briggs) was referring only to illegal immigration.

Dr. Hanson agreed with Dr. Holzer's arguments, and added that the important issue for a policy discussion was how to resolve the problem. Dr. Hanson stated that immigration policy was a very blunt instrument with which to improve the livelihoods of disadvantaged workers, and that even in the absence of illegal immigration there were many factors that negatively affected their opportunities and labor market outcomes. Also, he stated that even in the absence of illegal immigration, changes in the economy resulting from globalization and technological change, and conditions affecting inner cities, would also likely outweigh effects from immigration policy changes.[29] Dr. Jaynes reaffirmed his agreement with Dr. Hanson's remarks, and stated that changes in either public policy or immigration flows were low on his list of what could affect jobs and wages of native-born low-wage workers.

Commissioner Kirsanow observed that perceptions depend very much on context, referring specifically to his conversations with inner-city low-skill workers in Cleveland who believed that illegal immigration had a big impact on them. He asked the panelists whether the

---

[26] Briefing Transcript, pp. 40–41.

[27] Id. at 43.

[28] Id. at 43–44.

[29] Id. at 45–47.

perception of the problem had an effect on the workers, and whether ethnic networking limited opportunities for those outside the network.[30]

Dr. Briggs responded that if illegal immigrants in such great numbers were competing for the jobs of professors, lawyers, and doctors, the debate would not be occurring because public policy would already have demanded reform. But because many illegal immigrants go into low-income jobs, Dr. Briggs viewed policy makers as deciding that freshman economics (the law of supply and demand) does not apply. Dr. Briggs objected strongly to loading up a labor market with a big labor force that is not legally in the country. He said that while ethnic networking is illegal under the Civil Rights Act of 1964, sociology recognizes its strength, especially in finding employment.[31] Vice Chair Thernstrom observed that there has never been a black labor market network in the same sense as other ethnic networks.

Commissioner Kirsanow then asked Dr. Briggs about testimony on this topic that he had provided to the House of Representatives in 1999, and whether he had any policy prescriptions now that differed from those offered in that testimony. While he could not recall the specific testimony, Dr. Briggs responded that his views had not changed over the years. He advocated strict enforcement of employer sanctions, but noted also that possible solutions should include more than border enforcement, since 40 percent of illegal immigrants violate immigration laws by overstaying their visas. He emphasized his opposition to amnesty because it would perpetuate the problem, due to family reunification provisions that continue to bring in low-skilled immigrants.[32]

Commissioner Heriot then asked about the effect of the movement of capital across borders; specifically, if illegal immigration were to end immediately and low-skill wages went up, would capital then move away from some industries or cause industries to move jobs out of the country—in effect hiring from the same pool of workers but in their native countries. Dr. Holzer responded that it varied a great deal, depending on which sector of the economy. For instance, he noted that garment or textile industry jobs have already largely left the country, and many more would leave even without illegal immigration. Other low-skilled jobs could not leave, such as construction, retail, restaurant, and health care work, where the work has to be done locally. He cautioned, however, that mobility of capital across borders was only one force, and that equally important were other forces, such as improvements in technology that gave employers more choices of how to produce. This would result in employers investing in such improvements and reducing their dependence on low-wage labor. He suggested that over time, in the absence of illegal immigration, some jobs would see wages rise but many would not. He also warned that if there were dramatic reductions in the presence of illegal workers, the economic disruption to some of the affected sectors in the short run would be enormous.[33]

---

[30] Id. at 48–49.

[31] Id. at 49–51.

[32] Id. at 53.

[33] Id. at 54–56.

Dr. Hanson agreed, adding that if the experiment being considered was dramatic reduction in immigration for the purpose of creating jobs, there was a parallel to consider in the case of Mexico's liberalization of its foreign investment laws in the 1990s: There was a huge surge of investment by the United States in Mexico during that period, but nonetheless a continuing increase in Mexican immigration to the United States. Dr. Hanson concluded that the expected increase in capital spending following a halt in illegal immigration would likely increase jobs available to native-born workers or raise wages only somewhat.[34] Dr. Briggs objected, saying that Mexico had also devalued its currency dramatically after the passage of the North American Free Trade Agreement (NAFTA), which meant that low-wage workers would still earn more in the United States.

Dr. Jaynes agreed with Dr. Hanson that simply stopping all illegal immigration would not automatically result in a transfer of jobs to native-born workers, even in industries such as meat processing in Southern and Western states, because the formerly high wages were unsustainable for reasons unconnected to immigration. He gave the example of immigrant women working in household services, an occupation formerly filled by black women, and stated that even if immigrants were suddenly absent, there would not be an influx of black women into such occupations. His second example was the meat processing industries in Arkansas, Georgia, and Nebraska, in which high wages circa 1979 (approximately $22 an hour in today's prices) were, in his view, unsustainable even absent the influx of immigrant workers willing to accept lower wages. He argued that those jobs would have moved elsewhere, or there would have been changes in capital techniques and allocation if immigrants had not taken those jobs.[35]

Dr. Briggs disagreed, recounting instances in which immigration enforcement had forced employers to raise wages and thereby attract native-born workers, particularly in the meatpacking industry in the South. Dr. Jaynes said that that was precisely his point, that there would be higher wages, but that those wages were unsustainable. Dr. Briggs objected strongly to what he viewed as the use of public policy to drive down wages artificially. Dr. Jaynes agreed on that point, noting that this is indeed a civil rights issue, since such policy was being used to trample on the rights of all workers by driving down wages and avoiding employment rights.[36] Vice Chair Thernstrom asked whether "artificial" was the correct word. Dr. Briggs responded that it was, since deliberate failure to enforce the law was responsible for the wage suppression, and such action was indefensible. He also disagreed with the contention that black women would not do household service work. Dr. Jaynes again questioned the duration of any rise in wages, a point joined by Dr. Holzer. Dr. Holzer added that no one in the room was arguing in favor of illegal immigration, but the fact remained that it exists and that legal and illegal workers were complements rather than substitutes. He stated that there were benefits and costs to changing the current numbers of illegal workers, and that such change creates disruptions that are hard to predict.[37]

---

[34] Id. at 56–57.

[35] Id. at 57–59.

[36] Id. at 59–60.

[37] Id. at 61–64.

Commissioner Yaki objected to the focus on race, and asked the panel whether race in this particular debate was a proxy for lack of educational and job training opportunities. Dr. Hanson agreed that education was very much an issue, but stated that talking about the wage impact of immigration was not a statement about race, but necessary to an analysis of distributional impacts. He added that negative effects of immigration on wages of low-skilled workers were consistent with immigration raising overall gross national product, although those gains could be undone by importing low-skilled workers who use more in benefits and government services than they pay in taxes.[38]

Commissioner Yaki asked for views on whether our society has failed to provide blacks in inner cities with adequate education and job training and whether discrimination has had an effect as well. Dr. Holzer responded that extreme residential isolation affects where people live and go to school, and thereby the skills they bring to the labor market. He added that men of all racial groups with low skills have been negatively affected by illegal immigration, although behaviors such as unwed parenthood and child support obligations have hindered employment viability among low-skilled workers.[39]

Dr. Briggs addressed Commissioner Yaki's objection to discussing and collecting information about illegal versus legal immigration because of its potential to foster an "us" versus "them" attitude. Briggs pointed out that the only way to measure the impact of immigration was to collect and analyze data, and that every Western nation was a nation of immigrants, making immigration policy a central issue. Dr. Briggs viewed the quality of data in this case as problematic, but said that raising the immigration issue should not lead to accusations of racism to stifle important policy debates.[40] He reiterated his objection to illegal immigration because it undermines the integrity of U.S. immigration policy and violates public policies directed at ensuring a minimum wage and occupational health and safety standards by promoting unfair competition.

Vice Chair Thernstrom disagreed with the view that urban school systems are starved for money, since the per-pupil spending in those districts is much higher than the average in the rest of the country. Dr. Holzer responded that he did not make that claim, although there was evidence that pre-kindergarten educational programs would benefit from more funds. He claimed that better teachers were fundamental to improvement, but Vice Chair Thernstrom pointed out that getting better teachers had been attempted and failed, and that no one knew how to make it succeed.[41]

---

[38] Id. at 68–69. The Commission did not solicit testimony on the costs of social services or benefits to communities with large influxes of illegal immigrants, or the effect, positive or negative, of illegal immigration on urban social pathologies such as crime, disease, and overcrowding in high-immigration areas. *See, for example,* chapter three ("Immigrant Demands on Public Benefits") of *Why Does Immigration Divide America? Public Finance and Political Opposition to Open Borders*, by Dr. Gordon Hanson (Washington, DC: Institute for International Economics 2005).

[39] Id. at 72–73.

[40] Id. at 73–75.

[41] Id. at 80.

Commissioner Kirsanow noted that a number of people say that the effect of unwed motherhood in the black community is the principal civil rights issue, and that social pathologies flow from that. He asked if illegal immigration had a domino effect on rates of unemployment, wages, marriage, and incarceration in the black community, and, if so, to what extent. Dr. Holzer did not see direct links, but posited that illegal immigration could drive down wage and employment opportunities that, in turn, could affect the marriageability of black males. Commissioner Kirsanow asked if the competition for jobs between illegal workers and young workers robbed young people of the typical path of progressive employment. Dr. Holzer agreed that young black men probably do not see how they are going to get good jobs, and, as a result, may disengage from school, the labor market, and the mainstream society. He concluded, however, that low marriage rates, the disappearance of strong career and technical education, and the deterioration of job networks, among other factors, far outweighed immigration in limiting access to good jobs and wages.[42]

Dr. Briggs again disagreed that the size of the immigration effect justified the abandonment of immigration law enforcement. Dr. Jaynes responded that it was more important to address much bigger causative elements such as unwed motherhood and lack of education, which predated the growth in immigration.[43] Commissioner Kirsanow stated that births to unwed black mothers had grown from about 24 to 70 percent during the same period as the increase in immigration. Dr. Jaynes agreed with these growth figures, but disagreed that they occurred contemporaneously. He stated that the urban illegitimacy rate was already in the 40 percent range by the mid 1960s at the start of the great influx of immigration, and that fundamental attitudes responsible for the rise were formed already. Dr. Briggs added that the black female labor force exceeded that of black males, a statistic he found alarming.[44]

Panel Two

Julie Hotchkiss

Dr. Hotchkiss,[45] speaking on her own behalf, presented an economic analysis that she had undertaken with Myriam Quispe-Agnoli, currently a research economist and assistant policy adviser in the Latin America Research Group of the Federal Reserve Bank of Atlanta, which addressed three questions: 1) How are wages affected when the concentration of undocumented workers increases? 2) Is there any evidence that documented workers are displaced when firms fire a greater share of undocumented workers? and 3) Does the presence of undocumented workers exert more downward pressure on wages than the presence of legal immigrants?

According to Dr. Hotchkiss, this analysis, based on restricted data from the Georgia Department of Labor in administering Georgia's unemployment insurance program, can be generalized to the Commission's nationwide inquiry because Georgia had the fastest growth

---

[42] Id. at 80–83.

[43] Id. at 84.

[44] Id. at 84–85.

[45] Id. at 88–96.

in undocumented persons of any state between 2000 and 2006; is ranked sixth in the country for the size of the undocumented population; and is fourth in the nation for the size of the black population (30 percent of the state's population self-identifies as black). Dr. Hotchkiss's data set allowed her to distinguish between wages of documented and undocumented Georgia workers, to estimate movement within and outside of particular employment sectors and thus to quantify the effect of undocumented workers on documented workers, but did not include racial categories or information on workers' education levels.

Dr. Hotchkiss's data found dramatic growth of undocumented workers in expected sectors such as construction, leisure and hospitality, and services such as landscaping. She noted, however, that estimates by the Center for Immigration Studies suggest that her data set substantially undercounts the number of undocumented workers in Georgia primarily because it does not include workers not reported on official wage reports.

Dr. Hotchkiss performed several separate statistical analyses to isolate effects on wages from other effects such as job losses as a result of an influx of illegal immigrant workers. Her first statistical analysis considered the effects of undocumented workers on wages, holding all other factors constant. Given the increase in the share of undocumented workers in Georgia from 4 to 7 percent between 2000 and 2007, Dr. Hotchkiss found that the annual earnings of the average documented worker in 2007 were 2.9 percent or $960 lower than in 2000. In the leisure and hospitality industry, average documented worker earnings were 9.1 percent or $1520 lower than in 2000.

Dr. Hotchkiss's next statistical analysis showed that, holding all other factors constant including wages, an increase in a business's undocumented workers led to a decrease in the separation of documented workers. Instead, newly arrived undocumented workers displaced existing undocumented workers, suggesting greater substitutability among undocumented workers than between undocumented and documented workers. (The data could not distinguish between different types of separation—e.g., voluntary versus involuntary) She suggested that her analysis showed that newly arriving undocumented workers had no adverse effect on separation of documented workers.

Dr. Hotchkiss attributed this result to two forces. One is that the influx of undocumented workers exerted a downward pressure on wages, which led businesses to hire greater numbers of workers at lower salaries, in effect, substituting lower labor costs for capital expenditures. Second, businesses benefited from less expensive total production costs as a result of undocumented workers' smaller wages.

Finally, Dr. Hotchkiss observed that the impact of undocumented workers on wages is expected to be and, in her data, was greater than the impact of immigrants as a whole on wages. When workers, such as undocumented workers, do not have many alternative job prospects, Dr. Hotchkiss's analysis showed that they were only about half as likely as documented workers to leave their jobs in response to a lower wage. Businesses take advantage of this by paying lower wages. The sensitivity to wage changes varies considerably among documented workers, depending on their alternative job prospects. Generally, these workers are more responsive to such changes than undocumented workers.

Dr. Hotchkiss's conclusions were that 1) wages will be higher in the absence of undocumented workers; 2) employment will not necessarily be higher, and may even be lower, in the absence of undocumented workers; and 3) any effective policy that increases undocumented workers' employment and grievance rights will lead to higher wages for all workers on average.

Steven Camarota

Dr. Camarota,[46] a public policy analyst, agreed that illegal immigration increases the supply of workers in the low-skilled labor market, where black men are already disproportionately employed. He agreed, also, that in recent times, less-educated workers have fared relatively worse than better-educated workers, regardless of the measure—wages, benefits, or job security.

He reported on studies that looked at the impact of immigration generally, stating that the primary effect of immigration on wages and jobs comes about because of the increase in the supply of workers competing for the same jobs, which would be true regardless of their legal or illegal status. He did not view workers at that skill level as scarce.[47]

Dr. Camarota summarized the studies that discussed the effects of immigration on wages of minorities, and claimed that it is difficult to measure because we live in a national economy:

- A 1995 statistical analysis by Augustina Kposowa found that "non-whites appear to lose jobs to immigrants and their earning are depressed by immigrants."[48]
- A 1998 study by Howell and Mueller found that each 1 percent increase in the immigrant proportion of an occupation reduced wages for blacks in that occupation by about half a percentage point.[49]
- More recent research from Sum, Herrington, and Khatiwada found negative effects from immigration on less-educated natives overall, particularly on less educated minorities under the age of 30.[50]
- A qualitative study by anthropologists Newman and Lennon examining the fast food industry in Harlem indicated that immigrants had an advantage over native-born

---

[46] Id. at 96–104.

[47] *See also*, Steven Camarota, "Immigration Employment Gains and Native Losses, 2000-2004" in Debating Immigration at 139-156 (Carol Swain, ed., Cambridge Univ. Press, 2007); Steven Camarota, "Dropping Out: Immigrant Entry and Native Exit From the Labor Market, 2000-2005"(March 2006) (CIS Backgrounder), http://www.cis.org/articles/2006/back206 html (last accessed September 9, 2009).

[48] *See* Augustine J. Kposowa, "The Impact of Immigration on Unemployment and Earnings among Racial Minorities in the United States,"*Ethnic and Racial Studies*, vol. 18, no. 3 (July 1995).

[49] *See* David Howell, Elizabeth J. Mueller, "The Effects of Immigrants on African-American Earnings: A Jobs-Level Analysis of the New York City Labor Market, 1979-89" (November 1997), Levy Economics Institute Working Paper No. 210, available at http://ssrn.com/abstract=104648 or DOI: 10.2139/ssrn.104648.

[50] *See* Andrew Sum, Paul Harrington, and Ishwar Khatiwada (hereafter Sum, Harrington, and Khatiwada), "The Impact of New Immigrants on Young Native-Born Workers, 2000–2005," Center for Immigration Studies (Washington, DC: Center for Immigration Studies, September 2006), available at http://www.cis.org/articles/2006/back806.html.

blacks, and that this advantage almost certainly reflected the prejudices and biases of employers.[51]

- Other studies had not found an impact from immigration on blacks.

Dr. Camarota stated that the movement of labor and investment across cities creates an equilibrium that includes wages and employment, and as a result, studies looking at the country as one labor market have found a larger impact.

Dr. Camarota concluded that there is no debate that 1) immigration generally increases the supply of low-skilled workers; 2) a significant share of native-born blacks are more likely to be in labor competition with immigrants; and 3) employment and wages have declined for less-educated men. However, he believed that the question of whether immigration reduces wages or employment among black Americans was not entirely settled, but that if one is concerned about the prospects of less-educated workers in the country, it would be difficult to justify continuing high levels of immigration that disproportionately affect the bottom end of the labor market.

He noted a 1997 study, *The New Americans*,[52] conducted by the National Research Council, which found that immigration caused the poorest 10 percent of workers to lose about 5 percent of their wages, while the wages of the remaining workforce increased by 0.1 to 0.2 percent. As such, Dr. Camarota said that a central part of the immigration debate was how we weigh these benefits against the losses suffered by the poorest and least-educated Americans.[53]

Richard Nadler

Mr. Nadler[54] questioned the assumption of an oversupply of low-wage labor in analyzing the connection between immigration and unemployment of low-wage black workers. Focusing particularly on state-by-state trends from 2000 to 2007, Mr. Nadler matched the immigration patterns of the 50 states and the District of Columbia to data that immigration ostensibly affects, including gross state product, personal income, disposable income, median income, rates of poverty, unemployment, and crime.

Mr. Nadler's analysis examined what he termed "high immigration jurisdictions" ("HIJs"), meaning 1) states with the highest proportion of immigrants in their resident population, 2) high-influx states (those states whose population in 2007 was most altered as a percentage by an influx of immigrants since 2000), and 3) states with the highest number of foreign-born individuals, regardless of percentages. Together, these 19 states contained over 80 percent of the immigrant population, and about 60 percent of the native-born black population.

---

[51] *See* Katherine Newman, Chauncy Lennon, "Finding Work in the Inner City: How Hard is it Now? How Hard Will It Be for AFDC Recipients?" (Russell Sage Foundation Working Paper 76, Oct. 1995).

[52] *See* James P. Smith, Barry Edmonston, eds., *The New Americans: Economic, Demographic, and Fiscal Effects of Immigration*, National Research Council, (Washington, DC: National Academy Press, 1997).

[53] *See also*, "Sum, Harrington, and Khatiwada, "The Impact of New Immigrants on Young Native-Born Workers, 2000-2005 (CIS Backgrounder), http://www.cis.org/articles/2006/back806.pdf (accessed September 9, 2009).

[54] Briefing Transcript, pp. 104-112.

His analysis showed that the HIJs had gross state product growth that was significantly higher than in low-immigration jurisdictions (LIJs). According to Mr. Nadler, this ran contrary to the expectation that high immigration resulted in a decrease in gross state product because of a slow-down in capitalization per worker. He found that in HIJs, personal income per capita and median income were higher, personal income grew faster, and disposable income and disposable income per capita, whether measured in dollars or rates of increase, were higher. Based on a comparison of state and local tax rates in all 50 states and the District of Columbia, he concluded that the tax burden in the HIJs did not vary from that of the LIJs. He concluded that this finding undermined the assumption that high levels of immigration resulted in increased taxes to pay for the social services used by immigrants. He found that, in general, unemployment was lower in HIJs than in LIJs, and that the crime rates for HIJs were virtually identical to those in the LIJs.[55] His summary was that high levels of immigration correlated with above-average performance in the measures mentioned above and with below-average rates of individual and household poverty and unemployment.

Mr. Nadler next analyzed black unemployment data, and found that although black rates are higher than non-black rates, they were lower in HIJs than in LIJs. His data did not separate low-wage employment from black employment as a whole, but he examined state data on child poverty to find an analogy to low-wage employment effects among blacks. He found that child poverty rates among blacks in the HIJs was lower than both the national average and in the LIJs, although he noted that child poverty is not the same as household poverty. He concluded that the migration of labor to HIJs reflected a cause, not just an effect of prosperity. He expressed support for comprehensive immigration reform that would provide a path to legalization for illegal immigrant workers.

Carol Swain

Dr. Swain,[56] editor of *Debating Immigration*,[57] invoked the memory of Dr. Martin Luther King, Jr. and noted that this briefing occurred on the 40th anniversary of his assassination, a day on which he had gone to Memphis to support black sanitation workers on strike to protest poor working conditions. Dr. Swain referred to national surveys showing general support among all Americans for immigration reform, and observed that well-recognized problems that stem from illegal immigration affect the social, political and economic well-being of black and other Americans together. She also noted that it was important to find the systemic causes of black unemployment, which has not only been consistently greater than unemployment among the general population, but even rose at a time when unemployment among non-black workers fell.

Dr. Swain observed that a disproportionate number of black unemployed are high school dropouts. In addition, she stated that the 40 percent of the black population who are high school graduates were more adversely affected by the 2003 recession than members of other

---

[55] Id. at 108.

[56] Id. at 112-119.

[57] Debating Immigration, (Carol Swain, ed., Cambridge Univ. Press 2007).

racial and ethnic groups. Of those who are newly employed, the gains have more often occurred in low-wage, dead-end jobs.

Dr. Swain put forth several possible causes for high rates of black unemployment: 1) an oversupply of low-skilled workers, 2) racial discrimination by employers, and 3) inadequate education and training. She referred to figures developed by another panelist, Dr. Steven Camarota, which showed that new low-skilled immigrants have increased the supply of labor by 25 percent since 1990, and constituted 40 percent of workers without a high school diploma. This created competition among what she termed "people at the margins of society,"[58] a group that includes less-educated workers of all races generally. She believed that black males, however, faced more employment discrimination in general, and that employers preferred whites, even those with worse employment credentials than blacks. In her view, low-skilled workers of any race receive inadequate education as a result of cuts in state and federal education programs.

Dr. Swain concluded by stating that blacks are facing increased competition for jobs by immigrants that is unlikely to end. Dr. Swain also stated that black unemployment might be a contributing factor to neighborhood dysfunctions in the African-American community. These dysfunctions also include violent crime, single-parent households, illegitimacy, infant mortality, drug use, and infectious diseases. She recommended that an independent commission take on the responsibility of reforming immigration, making it costlier for employers to discriminate against native-born workers and increasing penalties for anyone in this country illegally. Investments in education, training, and a tamper-proof Social Security card, she said, would help protect all disadvantaged workers.

Discussion

Dr. Robert Lerner[59] asked for clarification of Dr. Hotchkiss's results. She responded that her statistical estimate of the impact of illegal workers in Georgia was greater than what other scholars found for immigrants as a whole—an expected result, she said, due to the absence of legal protections afforded illegal workers and the resulting financial advantages to employers. She added, however, that because there were fewer illegal workers than immigrant workers as a whole, the practical impact on wages was small, about 2.9 percent lower wages for workers generally, but was much larger (9 percent) in sectors such as leisure and hospitality that employed a larger share of illegal workers.[60] In response to another question from Dr. Lerner, Dr. Hotchkiss stated that 2.9 percent is about $960 on an annual basis, and 9 percent is about $1,500 annually.[61] Commissioner Yaki inquired as to the presence of unionization, and Dr. Hotchkiss answered that it was low in Georgia, as it was considered to be in all Southeastern states.

---

[58] Briefing Transcript, p. 117.

[59] Assistant Staff Director, Office of Civil Rights Evaluation, United States Commission on Civil Rights.

[60] Briefing Transcript, p. 120.

[61] Id. at 121–22.

Dr. Camarota pointed out that the National Research Council had estimated that immigration reduced wages of the poorest 10 percent of workers by about 5 percent, and that such reduced wages were similar in effect to a cut in the Earned Income Tax Credit of about 50 percent. He considered this reduction large.[62]

Mr. Nadler objected to using non-longitudinal skill levels (skill levels not measured over time) as a measure, since he did not view the labor market as a zero-sum pie; nor did he believe that skill-level categories captured actual large wage trends that showed gains in those areas with the most immigration. Dr. Camarota disagreed, referring to statistics showing that as immigrants move into an area, less-educated natives move out, and those who would have moved in, do not. For example, workers moved from the East during the 1960s and 1970s to Southern California, but as immigration greatly increased in Southern California, domestic migration to that area diminished considerably. Mr. Nadler agreed that there were labor flows on a nationwide basis, and concluded that it was not sound public policy to disrupt the natural flows of capital and labor throughout the economy, which is why the high-immigration jurisdictions that he studied showed higher median income.[63] Dr. Camarota found unconvincing Mr. Nadler's assertion that immigration contributed to higher median incomes, noting that Nadler's statistics are more likely a reflection that immigrants are more likely to be attracted to areas experiencing high employment growth.

Dr. Hotchkiss stated that most economic analyses that showed negligible or positive employment outcomes in high-immigration areas were good quality studies that controlled for self-selection. Dr. Camarota objected to this view, arguing that the gains to the economy as a whole were miniscule, and lowering the wages to the poor by even a small amount was substantial, since they had so little income. Mr. Nadler disagreed with Dr. Camarota entirely, reiterating his point that the unemployment data did not support that view.[64]

Dr. Swain described the perceptions of blacks and Hispanics, and also low-income whites, that immigration has hurt the American worker.[65] She said that the discussion should take account of the ethnic violence between blacks and Hispanics and how perceptions lead to violence. She also stated that black unemployment is a contributing factor to dysfunctional conditions in black communities, such as violent crime, single-parent households, illegitimacy, infant mortality, drug use, and infectious diseases, and that these are all loosely connected.

Mr. Nadler interjected that Dr. Hanson's research had been misrepresented to create resentment against immigrants.[66] Dr. Swain disagreed, stating that until recently, the discussion assumed that immigration was a win-win situation and that even black leaders and groups have not spoken up for low-skilled black workers.

---

[62] Id. at 123–24.

[63] Id. at 124–28.

[64] Id. at 128–30.

[65] Id. at 130–31.

[66] Id. at 132.

Commissioner Yaki disagreed with Dr. Swain's view, arguing instead that the issue of immigration effects is a proxy for the failure to discuss the plight of young men in inner cities for whom education and job training are unavailable, and that immigration was being made a scapegoat for such failures. Commissioner Yaki complained also that the Commission briefing itself was oversimplifying the issue.[67]

Dr. Swain disagreed with Commissioner Yaki, stating that one of the reasons she compiled her book, *Debating Immigration*, was that the discussion up to then had been one-sided on the part of the pro-immigration debaters, and that anyone in disagreement had been demonized.[68]

Vice Chair Thernstrom asked in what way the educational needs of ethnic minorities and working class whites in inner cities had not been addressed, considering that the amount of money spent per pupil in inner cities frequently was double the amount spent elsewhere.[69]

Dr. Swain answered that teachers who invest themselves in the students and encourage them are important, and also that it is important to offer alternatives, such as vocational training, for those who do not belong in college or on an academic track. Dr. Swain felt that community colleges should be available to all students and were under-valued as a resource. Vice Chair Thernstrom disagreed that community colleges are not available, but agreed that inner city students may not know of the existence of such colleges.[70]

Commissioner Melendez asked the panel whether economic research on this topic had been communicated to the public effectively, and whether the research had been misused to build anti-immigrant sentiment and other discriminatory messages. Mr. Nadler agreed that it had been misused. Dr. Swain disagreed, stating that the general public does not think about data or research, but instead looks at what they see around them.[71]

Dr. Camarota agreed with Dr. Swain that raising questions about illegal immigration and its potential impact on job competition and low income workers is received with hostility and accusations of bigotry, and also that the general public does not pay attention to research. Mr. Nadler stated that, to the contrary, it had been discussed on cable news channels extensively. Dr. Swain agreed with Dr. Camarota that it is difficult to hold views that are not politically palatable, and she felt pressure to conform her views to what is considered politically acceptable.[72]

Commissioner Heriot asked Mr. Nadler that, if economic boomtowns raised average wages, then why were they not attracting low-skilled labor from other more economically depressed

---

[67] Id. at 133–34.

[68] Id. at 136–38.

[69] Id. at 138.

[70] Id. at 142.

[71] Id. at 143.

[72] Id. at 144.

geographic areas. Mr. Nadler did not address that question, but observed only that mobility of labor is not dependent on the numbers of immigrants in the workforce.[73]

Vice Chair Thernstrom asked Mr. Nadler to clarify his testimony about crime rates. He stated that immigration is very far down on the list of factors that have some correlation with crime, so that high-influx states ranged from low to high crime, and low-influx states also ranged from low to high crime. Vice Chair Thernstrom pointed out that he had not controlled for other demographic factors that would distinguish those states. Mr. Nadler responded that the high immigration states had 60 percent of the black population and roughly half of the Hispanic population.[74]

In reference to Vice Chair Thernstrom's question about mobility of low-skilled labor, Dr. Swain observed that poor people cannot always afford to relocate to find jobs, and may lack good credit for such things as paying for a security deposit on housing. Therefore, when immigrants displace native-born workers, it is more difficult for such workers to find work elsewhere. Mr. Nadler again disagreed on the grounds that his unemployment data did not reflect this finding. Dr. Camarota pointed out that unemployment statistics are aggregates of all workers, not just low-wage workers, and the statistics are usually quite different for low-wage workers. In addition, those who have fallen entirely out of the workforce do not even show up in the statistics. He surmised that if illegal immigration decreased, those workers would attempt to get jobs. Dr. Swain then offered a personal view drawn from her own family: that to a low-skilled worker the paperwork and administrative requirements for obtaining required documentation are overwhelming. Dr. Camarota countered, observing that low-skill workers would probably be more likely to seek work if immigration were reduced and there was a scarcity of workers.[75]

---

[73] Id. at 146–49.

[74] Id. at 149–50.

[75] Id. at 150–54.

Statements

Gordon H. Hanson

University of California, San Diego and National Bureau of Economic Research

Immigration and Labor Market Outcomes for African-Americans

During the last several decades, there has been a dramatic rise in U.S. immigration. In 1970, 5 percent of the U.S. population was foreign born; by 2006, the foreign born population share was 12 percent. In terms of employment, immigrants now account for one out of every seven U.S. workers.

There is considerable interest in the impact of immigration on the U.S. labor market. Following the logic of economic theory, since immigration increases the supply of workers in the U.S. economy, it should put downward pressure on the wages of native labor. The adverse wage impacts are strongest for workers that compete most directly with immigrants for jobs. With over 30 percent of immigrants having less than a high school education, it is low skilled native workers who are likely to feel the greatest effects from immigration.

Among economists, there is disagreement about whether the data bear out the negative predictions of immigration for U.S. labor. Without rehashing this debate, I will share with you that my own view—based on extensive data analysis—is that immigration has lowered wages for native born U.S. high school dropouts. What I would like to focus on in my brief remarks today is some specific research I have done of the impact of immigration on the wages, employment, and incarceration rates of African-American men. This work was written jointly with George Borjas of Harvard University and Jeffrey Grogger of the University of Chicago. I will summarize the results of our recent National Bureau of Economic Research Working Paper, "Immigration and African-American Employment Opportunities: The Response of Wages, Employment, and Incarceration to Labor Supply Shocks."

Low skilled black men have had a rough past few decades in the U.S. labor market. The employment rate of African-American men fell from 75 percent in 1960 to 68 percent in 2000.[76] This stands in contrast to the contemporaneous decline from 87 to 85 percent among white men. The employment gap widened even more for low-skill persons: the employment rate of black high school dropouts fell from 72 to 42 percent, whereas it fell from 83 to 64 percent among white high school dropouts. The decline in labor market participation among black men was accompanied by a rapid increase in the number of black men in correctional institutions. In 1980, only 0.8 percent of black men (and 1.4 percent of black high school

---

[76] The "employment rate" gives the average fraction of weeks worked during the calendar year prior to the Census (the ratio of weeks worked, including zeros, to 52). The "incarceration rate" gives the fraction of persons who are institutionalized at the time of the Census.

dropouts) were incarcerated. By 2000, 10 percent of black men (and 21 percent of black high school dropouts) were incarcerated.[77]

A large body of academic research examines wage and employment trends for African-Americans. One strand emphasizes impacts of government programs, such as the Social Security disability program or the minimum wage, in driving black men out of the labor market. Another analyzes whether the decline in the real wage of low-skill workers discouraged low-skill black men from entering the labor market. A third examines whether black incarceration rates were shaped by the crack epidemic of the 1980s.

Remarkably, there is little work on the link between immigration and the employment and incarceration of black men. Immigration has disproportionately increased the number of low-skill workers in the United States, but, as I have mentioned, there is disagreement over whether this influx has adversely affected competing native workers. The conflicting evidence hinges crucially on the nature of the empirical exercise: studies that measure the impact of immigration by looking at wage trends across local labor markets tend to find small effects, while studies that examine the evolution of the national wage structure find large effects. Regardless of the geographic unit used to analyze the impact of immigration, any such impact would presumably be larger in the black workforce. (In fact, some of the early studies in this literature specifically attempted to measure the impact of immigration on black wages.)

In our research, we examine the relation between immigration and black employment outcomes. Our empirical analysis shows that immigration has indeed lowered the wage of blacks. Our main interest, however, is on the consequences of this reduction in market wages. In particular, has the immigration-induced reduction in the black wage encouraged some black men to exit the labor force and shift to crime?

Using data drawn from the 1960–2000 U.S. Censuses, we find a strong correlation between immigration and wages, employment rates, and incarceration rates for blacks. Our study suggests that a 10 percent immigrant-induced increase in the supply of a skill group is associated with a reduction in the black wage of 4.0 percent, a reduction in the black employment rate of 3.5 percentage points, and an increase in the black institutionalization rate of 0.8 percentage points. Among white men, the same increase in supply reduces the wage by 4.1 percent, but has much weaker employment and incarceration effects: a 1.6 percentage point reduction in the employment rate and a 0.1 percentage point increase in the incarceration rate. These correlations are found in both national and state-level data.

What do these estimates imply about the cumulative effect of recent immigration on African-American men? The economic adjustments unleashed by the large 1980–2000 immigrant influx, a labor supply shock that increased the number of workers in the United States by nearly 10 percent and the number of high school dropouts by over 20 percent, reduced the employment rate of low-skill black men by about 8 percentage points. Immigration, therefore, accounts for about 40 percent of the 18 percentage point decline in black

---

[77] Ignoring the prevalence of incarceration rates provides a very misleading picture of employment trends in the black population.

employment rates. Similarly, the changes in economic opportunities caused by the 1980–2000 immigrant influx raised the incarceration rate of black high school dropouts by 1.7 percentage points, accounting for about 10 percent of the 20 percentage point increase observed during that period. Although immigration played an important role, much of the decline in employment and increase in incarceration for the low-skill black population would have taken place even if the immigrant influx had been far smaller.

These potentially controversial findings can be easily misinterpreted. Although we have attempted to control for other factors that may account for the large shifts in black employment and incarceration rates over the 40–year period that we examine, no study can control for all possible factors. It is equally important to emphasize that although the evidence suggests that immigration played a role in generating these trends, much of the decline in employment or increase in incarceration in the black population remains unexplained.

In closing, suppose one believes our results that immigration has lowered wages and raised incarceration rates among black men. Does this mean that restrictions on immigration are called for? The short answer is no. Most economists believe that immigration, like international trade, has beneficial effects for the U.S. economy overall. An inflow of foreign workers allows U.S. technology, plant and equipment, and other resources to be used more productively, raising national income. Yet, while immigration benefits U.S. employers and consumers, we've seen that it harms some groups, including the low skilled. The appropriate policy response to immigration's negative effects would not be to restrict immigration, which would deny the U.S. economy the overall gains that foreign labor brings, but to seek ways to help the losers from immigration.

Gerald D. Jaynes

Professor of Economics and African American Studies, Yale University

Economic Effects of Immigration on Black Workers

Chairman Reynolds and members of the Commission, my name is Gerald Jaynes and I am Professor in the department of economics and in the department of African American Studies at Yale University. One of my major research interests during the past decade and a half has been immigration and its effects on race and ethnic relations and the economy. It is my pleasure to offer you my thoughts on the economic effects of immigration on the wages and employment of African American workers. My conclusions carry the weight of one whose views have been converted by objective evidence and personal research. Several years past, a colleague (Franklin Wilson—University of Wisconsin) and I were convinced that immigration had profound negative effects on the jobs and wages of African Americans. To ascertain the quantitative effect of immigration, we undertook a large scale statistical analysis of the U.S. labor market. Despite strong convictions for our hypothesis that immigration had large negative effects on black workers in particular, the data forced us to conclude otherwise: negative effects were mostly absent and modest at worst for only a small segment of lowest skilled workers.

Summarizing my views today, I know of no credible analysis separating the effects of documented and undocumented immigration, but the evidence supports the conclusion that from an economic standpoint immigration's broader benefits to the nation outweigh its costs. An assessment of the effects of immigration on the employment prospects of less educated native born black workers is that the effect is negative but modest, and probably is significant in some specific industries and geographic locations. A small set of specific labor markets are negatively impacted by undocumented immigration; important examples are meat packing in several areas of the South and Midwest and certain types of construction work throughout the nation. However, the relative importance of less educated black workers' job losses due to the competition of immigrants is swamped by a constellation of other factors diminishing their economic status. A significant minority of our most disadvantaged young people persist in low educational achievement, dropping out of high school, and engaging in negative behaviors such as criminal activity. Substantial improvement of the economic status of disadvantaged African American workers will require considerable change in their social status on many dimensions.

Labor Market Losers?

The charge that immigrants reduce the wages and employment of native-born black Americans is one of the most contentious issues of the debate over immigration. Despite the highly organized and publicly visible forces touting evidence of immigrants' devastating effects on native workers, and especially young black workers, how immigrant workers affect native labor markets remains a topic of uneasy debate among both lay people and economists. Some people argue current levels of immigration are literally destroying communities because undocumented workers are driving blue-collar wages so low a middle class standard of living is becoming unattainable for many working Americans. Such arguments often claim foreign workers are particularly detrimental to the job prospects of young African-American men lacking high school diplomas. Yet, according to polls, at least until very recently, possibly a majority of American citizens believes otherwise. Many Americans are more likely to believe immigrants fill jobs that without them would remain vacant and that their labor accelerates economic growth and expands overall employment.

Consistent with these polls, rigorous analyses of the effects of immigration on less-educated native workers suggests these effects are relatively small and in any event secondary to other causes of less educated native workers' often dismal employment experience. As I have commented elsewhere, in addition to an abundance of anecdotal evidence showing immigrant "takeover" of specific jobs (Jaynes, 2000:23), both common sense and straightforward economic reasoning explain why some Americans say they believe immigrants lower wages and displace native-born workers from jobs. The common sense behind these fears emerges from the most basic principles of supply and demand; mass immigration of millions of migrants looking for work in a new country should be expected to exert a large and negative effect on the wage and employment opportunities of workers already in the country. The strongest evidence concerns male employment, and we focus on it.

Recent Labor Market Experience of Black Males

Supply and demand theory is supported by the fact that the surge in immigration during the past 35 years occurred simultaneously with a large drop in the inflation-adjusted wages of less-educated American workers. The adverse trend in the wages of less educated men in particular was both absolute and relative to the wages of college educated men (Jaynes, 2006). As the average education levels of arriving immigrants declined significantly after 1980, the compensation of less-educated U.S. workers fell dramatically relative to wages of the highly educated. One way to understand the increases in earnings inequality is to compare the earnings of high school and college graduates. The earnings of full-time high school graduate men fell significantly compared to the earnings of college graduate men of the same age. Underlying the disadvantageous change in high school men's relative wages were two basic trends; while the inflation adjusted earnings of college graduates increased significantly after the mid-seventies, the inflation adjusted earnings of high school graduates at best stagnated and at times declined.

The largest reductions in earnings occurred among less educated men and women and for all races. During the decade and a half period encompassed by the early 1970s and the late 1980s, the earnings of the poorest 10 percent of working men fell more than 30 percent even as the earnings of the most affluent 40 percent held steady. To illustrate the point, between the years 1969 and 1984 (measuring in 1984 constant dollars) the mean weekly wages of white male high school graduates fell from $481 to $393; this was a reduction of 18 percent. The fall in mean weekly earnings among white male high school dropouts was much sharper; 37 percent. Sharp reductions in the already lower wages of comparably educated African American men decimated working conditions among young black males. During this fifteen year period, black male high school graduates' mean weekly wages fell 22 percent from $357 to $278, and for black male dropouts mean weekly wages were in a period of free fall, dropping 32 percent from $312 to $213.

Falling inflation-adjusted wages and rising earnings inequality were accompanied by increasing male joblessness, and as any one remotely familiar with the recent socioeconomic history of the United States knows, joblessness and low earnings were especially severe among young black males. Deteriorating wage opportunities had already precipitated severe reductions in young black men's employment during the decade of the 1970s, but their labor market position deteriorated even further during the 1980s. Overall, the unemployment rate of black men exceeded 20 percent during the early 1980s. At the midpoint of the eighties decade, the average black man aged 20 to 24 who had dropped out of high school earned only $146 per week when employed, unfortunately such black men had an unemployment rate of 45%. Their high school graduate counterparts fared little better, averaging earnings of $165 per week. White dropouts that age earned a third more and faced half the unemployment rate, a situation still burdensome for their communities. The response to these catastrophically low wages was a marked detachment of many black men from legal market employment. Thus, although in 1970, black high school graduates and college graduates ages 25–34 had similar employment rates (90 percent versus 90.4 percent), by 1985 high school graduates had an employment rate 13 percentage points lower (66.3 percent versus 79.6 percent). The employment rate of same age black high school dropouts during 1985 was 57.2 percent, more than 20 points lower than the college graduates. During 1970, even the dropouts had enjoyed an employment rate of 85 percent. An indicator of the extent to which these young men took recourse through black and gray market work is that the proportion of black high school dropouts in this age group reporting no earnings more than tripled, from 7 percent in 1970 to 23 percent in 1985.

More recent labor market experience of young American men has continued to bolster the claims of critics of immigration who say immigration deteriorates the employment prospects of African American males. While the wages of full-time working white and Latino male high school graduates rose sharply during the economic boom between 1995 and 2000, the wages of similar black men were flat, leading many people to speculate that heavy Latino immigration during this period was indeed deteriorating employment and wage opportunities for black men. See Figure 1, which also illustrates the general deterioration in the wages of young white and Latino men since 2000. The fact that the wages of young Latino men overtook the wages of similar young black men during this period merely flames the fires of discontent over immigration.

Assessing the Evidence of Immigration's Labor Market Effects

One need not search hard to find disturbing evidence that recent immigrants may exert negative effects on sectors of the U.S. labor market. But how convincing is the evidence? Social scientists require stronger proof than mere correlation between arriving numbers of immigrants and deteriorating job market conditions for natives. After all, the last four decades of U.S. history have encompassed a host of socioeconomic changes, each of which offers an alternative explanation for the deteriorating economic circumstances of lower skilled black workers. The specifics of the alternatives make the conjecture especially salient for young black males. No remotely credible argument blames immigration for the large and near steady reduction in blue-collar jobs in the U.S. which began during the 1950s. Nor did immigration cause the weakening of labor unions, automation, growth of the computerized information economy, or deteriorating U.S. import-export balances that suck up good paying jobs.

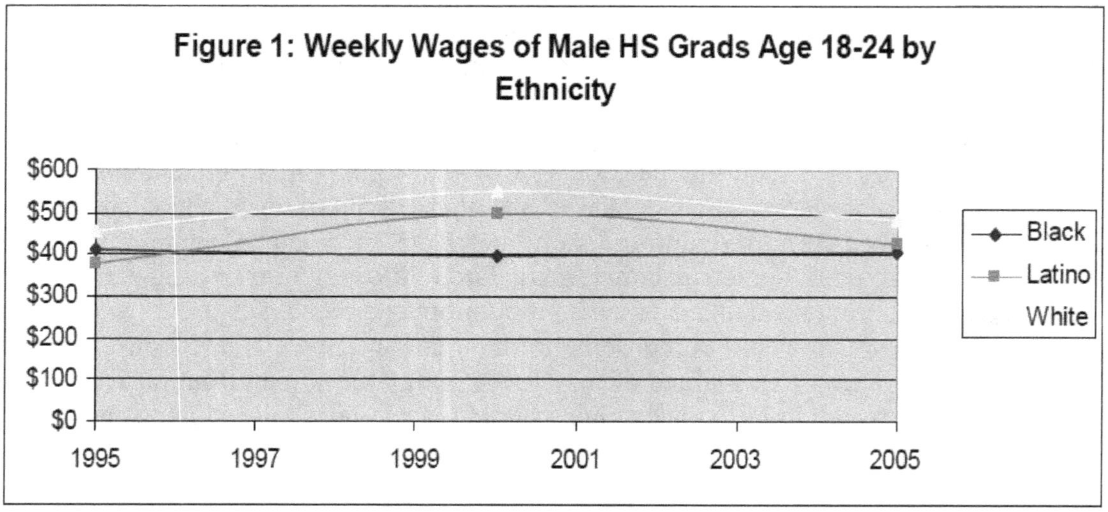

Figure 1: Weekly Wages of Male HS Grads Age 18-24 by Ethnicity

A line chart titled "Figure 1: Weekly Wages of Male HS Grads Age 18-24 by Ethnicity" with the vertical axis marked from $0 to $600 in $100 increments, and the horizontal axis marked with years 1995, 1997, 1999, 2001, 2003, 2005. The legend identifies three series: Black, Latino, and White.

Data calculated from CPS Annual Social and Economic Supplement, 2006, Table PINC-04; 2001 March Supplement, Table PINC-04; 1996, Table PINC-06A. Wages of Full-time workers are annual earnings divided by 52.

And, indeed, social scientists' rigorous statistical analyses initially stood upon its head the common sense of straightforward supply and demand theory. Until well into the 1990s, the great preponderance of rigorously designed and executed studies of immigration's effects on the economic position of U.S. citizens concluded that the effects were either ambiguous and in any case negligible or that immigrants in fact had a positive effect on the employment and wages of natives. These results held for both skilled and unskilled native-born workers and for women, minorities, and whites. The one demographic group providing an exception to the findings of no negative effects was recent Latino immigrants, who were found to be hurt by those who arrived behind them.

The counterintuitive results of this research were explained in the following terms. The job skills brought into the country by less-educated immigrants were complementary to the skills of higher educated and trained natives; therefore immigrants did not compete for natives' jobs. On the contrary, the rising supply of immigrant workers ready and able to work hard for low wages is said to spur the expansion of many existing firms and the growth of new firms able to profit from the low wages. The expanding firms based on low wage immigrant labor also hired more skilled native labor as their revenues grew. Janitorial services, car washes, landscapers, and poultry processing plants with growing numbers of employees require more supervisors, clerical workers, accountants, etc. Using this literature, proponents of immigration argued that immigrants in fact improved the working position of natives.

More Recent Analyses

Dissatisfaction with the statistical methods used in early studies of the effects of immigration on the employment opportunities of natives led to the use of different models. Using more sophisticated statistical methods than the earlier literature, Borjas, Freeman, and Katz (1992) estimated that during the 1980s increased imports of goods produced with lower-skilled labor and rising immigration of lower-skilled labor were important contributors to the adverse turn in the weekly wages of American high school dropouts as they compared to the weekly wages of American college graduates. These authors estimated the "implicit" increase in the supply of lower-skilled labor within the U.S. that is consistent with the increased volume of U.S. imports and immigrant labor supply. They estimated 30 percent to 50 percent of the decline in the relative weekly wage of high school dropouts between 1980 and 1988 should be attributed to increased immigration and trade. Wilson and Jaynes (2000:22-3) decomposed the effects of immigration on geographic labor markets into separate effects of flows and stocks of immigrant workers. Their analysis also estimated separate effects for various native-born ethnicities and skill-education groups. They found that immigration flows across geographic areas were a negligible factor on the declining wages and employment of less educated native born workers. That finding is consistent with the no effects findings of earlier literature. However, they also found that the size of the immigrant population within a given area did have a modest negative affect on the employment of less educated African Americans.

More recently, Borjas and Katz (2005) have refined earlier methods even further and updated analysis of the effects of Mexican immigration on low skilled workers to cover the 1990s. They conclude that the large growth in immigration during the eighties and nineties (particularly the acceleration of low-skilled Mexican laborers) lowered the wages of native-born high school dropouts by about 8 percent and exerted a modest influence in widening overall wage inequality within the U.S (2005: 37-38,Table 11, p. 63).

Special Labor Markets

Despite the relatively modest effects on natives' wages in the U.S. overall, there are obviously some job markets where immigrants exert significant influences on natives' job prospects. Meatpacking is a salient example of an industry where case study provides strong evidence that low-wage undocumented immigrant workers have displaced native-born workers. Always an especially dirty, physically demanding, and often dangerous occupation, meatpacking jobs have historically attracted only the least educated members of the workforce. The industry has typically offered employment to large numbers of African Americans. Today immigrants dominate jobs in meatpacking and the undocumented are a significant force. During the late nineties, the Immigration and Naturalization Service estimated that undocumented workers composed 25 percent of the labor in meatpacking plants in Iowa and Nebraska. During the past two decades, immigrant labor has come to dominate the poultry industry in the Southern states. In these earliest years of the 21st century, Latino immigrants are about three-fourths of the workers in the poultry plants located in Northwest Arkansas, the vast majority of the remaining workers are from Southeast Asia and the Marshall Islands. Native-born workers are now rare.

Through the 1970s and into the eighties, larger meat packing firms were heavily unionized with nearly one-half (46 percent) of the industry's workers unionized. The larger unionized plants paid a wage premium, and during 1982 the base wage rate of the largest union was $10.69 per hour ($22.33 per hour in terms of 2006 inflation adjusted prices). Rapid immigration of workers from Southeast Asia, Mexico, and Central America during the 1980s coincided with firm demands that workers accept wage cuts. Extremely turbulent employer-union relations in terms of strikes and corporate attacks on unions characterized the 1980s.

During the period 1983–1986 there were 158 work stoppages involving some 40,000 workers in cattle and hog plants. By 1987, the union percentage of the workforce had been cut to 21 percent, and wages were down to the $8 to $9 range in union and non-union plants. A sharp decrease in workers' health and safety accompanied the collapse of the unions. Even though the meatpacking industry already had the highest rates of occupational injuries and illness of all U.S. industry, on the job illness and injury rates peaked in 1991 at 45.5 per 100 workers. Jobs in the industry deteriorated so badly that only the steady influx of cheap immigrant labor compensated for the extraordinarily high turnover rates, reaching as high as 100 percent annually at some plants during the 1990s. Under these conditions, it is true that meatpacking plants have difficulties attracting native workers (Macdonald, et al, 1999:15-16).

Further Policy Directions

What are the policy implications of findings that low-skill immigrants lower the employment opportunities of some less educated native workers? If the United States allocates much larger resources to border security to significantly reduce the number of undocumented workers while also tightening legal channels of immigration, would the reduction in immigrant workers result in more and higher pay jobs for American citizens? The easy answer is that the reduced labor supply would indeed raise wages and allow more employment of the native-born. However, as with any question of economic effects, the demand side of the equation must also be considered. Undocumented workers with few legal protections take jobs for lower pay and do them under more undesirable working conditions. Such immigrant workers lower employers' costs. Take away the immigrants and the result will be increased costs and lower business profits. Where possible, a greater proportion of jobs will be outsourced. Some of the more marginal businesses that will have to pay higher wages to workers who are not as productive will not survive, and the demand for less educated workers will likely decrease. The net effect is that wages and employment of native-born workers will likely rise, but not nearly as much as a simple comparison of raw numbers suggests.

Low-wage labor conditions unbecoming an affluent democratic society exist because in the present climate of immigrant bashing there is little support for social and political action saying let's protect illegal workers. But this is short sighted, ultimately, if working conditions are allowed to deteriorate to levels where migrants are exploited, all labor with whom the migrants compete become exploited as well. This is true even if natives' exploitation materializes in the form of joblessness and poverty. The terms of the debate must be changed to a desire to protect the integrity of the nation's low-wage labor markets and the citizens working in them from conditions inconsistent with standards of living and values of justice in affluent representative democracies.

It is crucial that the nation adopt social policies designed to protect the rights and living standards of all low wage workers. Such policies need not require draconian migration polices that ban immigrants. Indeed, the worldwide globalization of markets ensures such migration will continue. However, migration must be better regulated to ensure numbers consistent with work conditions appropriate to the living standards in host countries. Wages consistent with standards of decency for the least remunerated workers will need to be supported by a program of explicit policies and reforms:

- minimum wage laws covering all workers

- enhancement of earnings by expanding the current Earned Income Tax Credit system to all citizen households who work fulltime

- documented immigrant workers must be guaranteed reasonable paths to citizenship

- protection of low wage markets through stronger enforcement of existing laws against undocumented migration

There are costs to instituting these policies. If employment conditions and compensation are increased enough to attract citizen workers, employers' profits will fall, and prices of some services and products will rise. This will necessarily raise strong opposition to these policies from obvious political constituencies. The simple fact that high migration of poor low skilled workers into more affluent geographic regions raises the profits of employers of less-educated workers explains why employers continue to clamor for more migrants and guest workers (documented or not). In so far as middle class households employ such labor to clean houses, landscape, do repair work or consume products and services priced lower because of the cheap labor, a wide spectrum of middle class and affluent citizens gain economically from migration. Other interest groups demand an end to all immigration, claiming the migrants are devastating the employment prospects of young, less educated native workers and depriving poor unassimilated minorities the opportunity to work themselves into the lower middle class.

On average, Americans receive positive economic benefits from immigration, but, at least in the short run, residents of particular localities and members of certain groups may lose. Cost benefit analysis is only concerned with a comparison of aggregate costs and benefits; who bears the costs is not considered. But in any large-scale social reorganization, there are inevitably winners and losers. Economists call the welfare principle that legitimates cost-benefit analysis as a decision-making criterion for social policy the Hicks Compensation Principle. Stated succinctly, it merely says that if aggregate benefits of immigration exceed costs, the gains of all society's winners are sufficient to adequately compensate all society's losers. In theory, such payments from winners to losers would make everyone better off. In practice, such compensation is seldom forthcoming. Along with localities hosting disproportionately few immigrant residents but benefiting from the employment of many immigrant workers, owners of capital, and most consumers and workers gain at the expense of some native-born workers. The losers are low-skilled, poorly paid, and disproportionately minority.

Democratic concepts of justice suggest the losses of a few should not override the gains of the many. Democratic concepts of justice also demand that society's least advantaged members should not be paying for the immigration benefits enjoyed by the entire nation. A democratic society benefiting from immigration and debating how to reshape its immigration policies should also be discussing social policies to compensate less-skilled workers through combinations of better training, relocation, and educational opportunities. It should also be debating how the federal government should address the unequal burdens of immigration among localities.

Citations

Borjas, George, Richard B. Freeman, and Lawrence F. Katz. "On The Labor Market Effects of Immigration and Trade," in Richard B. Freeman and George Borhas eds, *Immigration and the Workforce, Economic Consequences for the United States and Source Areas.* Chicago: U. Chicago Press, 1992.

Borjas George J. and Lawrence F. Katz "The Evolution of the Mexican-Born Workforce in the United States," Working Paper 11281, NBER, Cambridge, Mass: April, 2005.

Human Rights Watch, *Blood, Sweat, and Fear: Workers Rights in U.S. Meat and Poultry Plants, 2004,* http://hrw.org/reports/2005/usa0105/index.htm.

Jaynes, Gerald D. *Race and Immigration: New Dilemmas for American Democracy.* New Haven, Ct.: Yale University Press, 2000.

Jaynes, Gerald D. Two Evolutions: Black Affluence, Black Poverty—The Economics of African American Citizenship Since Emancipation. Manuscript, Yale University, 2006.

MacDonald, J., M. Ollinger, K. Nelson, and C. Handy. 1999. "Consolidation in U.S. Meatpacking." *Agricultural Economic Report 785.* Washington, D.C.: Economic Research Service, USDA.

U.S. Census Bureau, Press Release, May 10, 2006.

Wilson, Franklin D. and Gerald D. Jaynes, "Migration and the Employment and Wages of Native and Immigrant Workers," *Work and Occupations*, Vol. 27 No. 2, May 2000.

Vernon M. Briggs, Jr.

Emeritus Professor of Labor Economics, Cornell University

Illegal Immigration: The Impact on Wages and Employment of Black Workers

Overall Perspective

Before addressing the specific issue of illegal immigration and its economic effects on black Americans, the broad subject needs to be placed in perspective. No issue has affected the economic well-being of African Americans more than the phenomenon of immigration and its related policy manifestations. Immigration defined the entry experience of the ancestors of most the nation's contemporary black American community (as slaves who were brought as involuntary immigrants); it placed them disproportionately in the states that today comprise the "South"(at no point in American history has less than half the black population ever lived outside the South); it disproportionately tied them for centuries to the rural sector of the Southern economy, where they were linked with the region's vast agricultural economy (the black migration out of the South did not begin until after 1915, when the mass immigration of the late 19th and early 20th Centuries from Europe and Asia were cut off by war from 1914–1918 and by restrictive legislation from 1921–1965); and, with the accidental revival of mass immigration in the years since 1965 that has continued to this day, immigration has served largely to marginalize the imperative to address squarely and affirmatively the legacy of the denial of equal economic opportunity that had resulted from the previous centuries of slavery and segregation, which the civil rights movement and legislation of the 1960s sought to redress. In this post-1965 era of mass immigration, no racial or ethnic group has benefited less or been harmed more than the nation's African American community.

From 1965 to 2007, the foreign-born population of the United States has soared from 8.4 million persons to 39.3 million persons (from being 4.4 percent of the nation's population to being 12.7 percent). As for origin of this current wave of mass immigration, only 2.5 percent of the nation's foreign born population in 2000 (when the last Census was conducted) were from Africa [whereas 51 percent were from Latin America (including Mexico and Central America); 25.5 percent were from Asia; and 15.3 percent were from Europe; and the residual from Canada, Australia, New Zealand and various Pacific Islands]. Indeed, by 2004, the surge in immigration led to the replacement for the first time in the nation's history of black Americans as the nation's largest minority group by Hispanics, who now hold that distinction. Although black Americans were 13.5 percent of the nation's native–born population, they were only 7.8 percent of the foreign-born population in 2000. Hispanics, on the other hand, were only 8.5 percent of the native-born population while being 45.2 percent of the foreign-born population.

Illegal Immigration and the Low Wage Labor Market

A major explanation for the rapid growth of the nation's post-1965 immigrant population has been—and continues to be—illegal immigration. It is estimated that there are ll.3 million illegal immigrants in the country as of 2007 (plus another 1.1 million persons who are believed to be undercounted in the published estimates). This means that about 30 percent of the total foreign-born population are illegal immigrants. When one recalls that there have been seven amnesties given by Congress since 1986 that have legalized the status of over 6 million former illegal immigrants, it is not too much of a stretch of the imagination to conclude that upwards of half the current foreign-born population of the country entered in violation of the nation's immigration laws.

The most distinguishing characteristic of the illegal immigrant population is their paucity of human capital. It is currently estimated that 57 percent of the adult illegal immigrant population have not completed high school while an additional 24 percent have only a high school diploma. Thus, less than 19 percent of the illegal immigrant adult population have more than a high school education as of 2007. Since most illegal immigrants come from some of the world's poorest nations, the quality of the education received is likely to be poor as well, which means that the low levels of educational attainment are only part of the story.

Because of the low levels of human capital and the fact that they often lack adequate English-speaking skills, the vast majority of illegal immigrant workers are employed in low skilled occupations. Even those few with higher skills are often forced to work in the low skilled sector because their illegal status means that they often cannot use their credentials to get better jobs. Thus, the estimated 7.4 million illegal immigrant workers (who are about one-third of the total foreign-born labor force) compete for jobs and income with the other 43 million adult members of the low skilled labor force who are legally entitled to work in the civilian labor force (i.e., native born workers and the remainder of the foreign-born workforce who are naturalized citizens, permanent resident aliens, and non-immigrants with visa authorizations to work) in 2007.

In part due to the large supply of workers who comprise the low skilled labor force of the United States and in part due to the fact that higher skilled workers can (and often do) also work in this low skilled sector when they cannot find jobs for their talents, the low skilled labor market always has the highest level of unemployment of any of the segments of the U.S. labor force for whom educational attainment is measured. In February 2008, for instance, the national unemployment rate was 4.8 percent, but the unemployment rate for adults (over 25 years old) without a high school diploma was 7.3 percent. Low skilled adults also often must compete with youth who seek employment in large sectors of the unskilled labor market. Youths usually lose in this competition for jobs as employers typically prefer adults, who are more dependent on the labor market for their income than are young people. The unemployment rate for youth 16–19 years old was 16.8 percent and for young adults 20–24 years old was 8.9 percent in February, 2008.

Black Employment in the Low Skilled Labor Market

Of the 50 million low skilled adults (those 25 years of age and over) in the civilian labor force in 2007, black Americans accounted for about 5.6 million of such workers (or about 10 percent of the total). These black American workers, however, had the highest unemployment rates of any of the four racial and ethnic groups for which the data was collected. Black American adult workers without a high school diploma had an unemployment rate of 12.0 percent, and those with only a high school diploma had an unemployment rate of 7.3 percent in 2007. These 5.6 million low skilled black workers accounted for one-third of the entire black labor force of slightly over 17 million workers.

Black youths (16–19 years old) also had the highest unemployment rate of any of the racial groups for whom data is collected. Their unemployment rate for February 2008 was an astounding 31.7 percent. These data are, of course, only for those still actively seeking employment and who are not institutionalized. They do not include those who have been discouraged from seeking employment because they feel it would not be worthwhile even to try to find a job under these conditions of high unemployment among their peers. Nor do they include any of the more than 1 million black youth and adults who are incarcerated in the nation's penal system (often because of the inability to find regular employment).

Clearly, black American workers who are poorly skilled have the greatest difficulty finding jobs of all such workers similarly situated in the U.S. labor force.

Illegal Immigration and Black Workers

Illegal immigrant workers tend to concentrate in labor markets that have high concentrations of legal immigrants and citizens (native born and naturalized who are from similar ethnic and racial backgrounds). It is more difficult for authorities to identify them under these circumstances, and they can rely on networks of friends and family members as well as other employers and community assistance organizations composed of members of their same backgrounds to find employment. As a consequence, there is a tendency for illegal immigrants to cluster in metropolitan areas (especially central cities) or in rural areas that already have concentrations of persons from similar backgrounds.

Black workers also tend to be concentrated in metropolitan areas—especially in central cities. The only rural labor markets where black Americans are of significant number are in the Southeastern states—a legacy of the slavery heritage of yesteryear.

Thus, it is not everywhere that there is likely to be significant competition between low skilled black workers and illegal immigrant workers, but there are ample circumstances where there is—such as the large metropolitan labor markets of Los Angles, New York, San Francisco, Chicago, Miami and Washington-Baltimore. Moreover, some of the fastest growing immigrant concentrations are now taking place in the urban and rural labor markets of the states of the Southeast—such as Georgia, North Carolina and Virginia, which never before were significant immigrant receiving states in previous eras of mass immigration. Indeed, about 26 percent of the nation's foreign-born population are now found in the states of the South—the highest percentage ever for this region. There is mounting evidence that many of these new immigrants in this region are illegal immigrants.

Because most illegal immigrants overwhelmingly seek work in the low skilled labor market and because the black American labor force is so disproportionately concentrated in this same low wage sector, there is little doubt that there is significant overlap in competition for jobs in this sector of the labor market. Given the inordinately high unemployment rates for low skilled black workers (the highest for all racial and ethnic groups for whom data is collected), it is obvious that the major looser in this competition are low skilled black workers. This is not surprising, since if employers have an opportunity to hire illegal immigrant workers, they will always give them preference over legal workers of any race or ethnic background. This is because illegal immigrant workers view low skilled jobs in the American economy as being highly preferable to the job opportunities in their homelands that they have left. A job that pays the federal minimum wage of $7.15 an hour (some states and localities have even higher minimum wages) is often several times higher than the daily wage they could earn in their homelands, if they could get a job at all. Even the worst working conditions in the United States are typically better than what many have experienced before they came to this country. Illegal immigrants, therefore, are often grateful to receive these low wages, and they will do whatever it takes to get these jobs (even if it means living in crowded and substandard living conditions and working under harsh and dangerous conditions). It is also easier for some employers to exploit illegal immigrant workers by paying them less than the minimum wage and not paying them overtime wages because they are fearful of revealing their vulnerable status if they were to complain. Citizen workers know that paying the minimum wages means that the employer values your work at the lowest level that he/she can legally pay. Furthermore, citizen workers expect labor and safety laws to be enforced because they believe they have legal rights to job protections. It is not that citizen workers will not do the work that illegal immigrants are willing to do. Rather, it is that citizens often will not do the work for the same pay and under the same working conditions as will illegal immigrants—nor should they.

It is not that employers are evil in their willingness to give preference to illegal immigrants. It is that they are pragmatic in their decision making. Illegal immigrants are available because the federal government has chosen to do little to monitor the work sites of the nation. Seldom are any penalties placed on employers who violate the ban against hiring illegal immigrants working even though it has existed since 1986. Moreover, because of this self-imposed impotence by the federal government, employers who try to follow the law are penalized because they must compete with employers who violate the law and benefit by paying lower wages and providing cheaper working conditions that are more profitable to these employers but hazardous to the illegal workers. The status quo, therefore, is a perversity of justice. Law breakers are rewarded while law abiders are punished.

Economists long ago have realized that there is no way to prove or to measure the job displacement of citizens by illegal immigrants. This is because when immigrants (including the large illegal immigrant component) move into a local labor market, citizens tend to move out. Mass immigration has affected the internal migration patterns of citizen workers. As they leave the area or as they drop out of the labor market because they cannot find jobs, immigrants move in to claim the jobs But there is no way to measure the loss since many of the victims are no longer in the local labor market.

As for wage suppression, all studies show that the large infusion of immigrants has depressed the wages of low skilled workers. It is the illegal immigrant component of the immigration flow that has most certainly caused the most damage, but there is no way to isolate their singular harm. But even these studies most likely underestimate the true adverse impact because there is a floor on legal wages set by minimum wage laws that do not allow the market to set the actual wage level. What is known is that wages in the low wage labor market have tended to stagnate for some time. It is not just that the availability of massive numbers of illegal immigrants depress wages, it is the fact that their sheer numbers keep wages from rising over time, and that is the real harm experienced by citizen workers in the low skilled labor market.

What is apparent is that the unemployment rates in the low skilled labor market are the highest in the entire national labor force. This means that the low skilled labor market is in a surplus condition. Willing workers are available at existing wage rates. By definition, therefore, illegal immigrants who are overwhelmingly present in that same labor market sector adversely affect the economic opportunities of legal citizen workers because the illegal workers are preferred workers. No group pays a higher penalty for this unfair competition than do low skilled black Americans, given their inordinately high unemployment levels

The willingness of policy makers to tolerate the presence of illegal immigrants in the nation's labor force exposes a seamy side of the nation's collective consciousness. Illegal immigrants—who themselves are often exploited even though they may not think so—are allowed to cause harm in the form of unemployment and depressed wages to the most vulnerable workers in the American workforce. The continued reluctance by our national government to get illegal immigrants out of the labor force—and to keep them out—by enforcing the existing sanctions at the work site against employers of illegal immigrants is itself a massive violation of the civil rights of all low skilled workers in the United States and of low skilled black American workers in particular. Illegal immigrants have no right to work in the United States. In fact, they have no right to even be in the country. Enforcing our nation's labor laws—including the protection of the legal labor force from the presence of illegal immigrant workers—is the civil rights issue of this generation of American workers.

It is time, therefore, to make our immigration laws credible. The way to do this is to adhere to the findings of the U.S. Commission on Immigration Reform chaired by the late Barbara Jordan, who boldly stated what should be the goal of public policy: "The credibility of immigration policy can be measured by a simple yardstick: people who should get in, do get in; people who should not get in, are kept out; and people who are judged deportable, are required to leave."

No one would benefit more by the adherence to that standard than would low skilled black American workers and their families.

Harry J. Holzer

The Effects of Immigration on the Employment Outcomes of Black Americans

I'd like to address the question of how immigration—whether legal or illegal—affects the labor market opportunities and outcomes of native-born African-Americans. In doing so, I'd like to make several points.

- Most econometric evidence suggests that immigration over the past few decades has had a modest negative effect on the employment outcomes of blacks, especially those without high school diplomas.

The strongest evidence of negative effects comes from work by Borjas, Grogger and Hanson (2006). They find quite strong negative effects on the wages and employment of black male high school dropouts, and somewhat less on these outcomes for high school graduates, plus very small impacts on black incarceration rates for either group.[78]

This evidence is based on some quite strong statistical assumptions, and only considers the effects of immigration in the short-run—in other words, before capital inflows have occurred that would mitigate the negative impacts of immigrants on native-born workers. It is therefore likely that the these estimates overstate any real negative impacts, even though some of these estimates themselves are already small.[79]

But the notion that there are at least some negative effects is bolstered by some newer papers that have been written more recently. For instance, Deborah Reed and Sheldon Danziger (2007) also find some very modest negative effects of immigration on the employment of black men, using a simpler methodology that compares outcomes across metropolitan areas. In an MIT doctoral dissertation, Christopher Smith (2008) has found somewhat larger negative effects on the employment rates of both white and black teens, but much more modest effects as they age into their 20s.[80] These papers are significant, because analysis of

---

[78] For instance, their estimates suggest that immigration between 1980 and 2000 has reduced wages by 8.3 percent, reduced employment by 7.4 percentage points, but raised incarceration by only 1.7 percentage points among black male high school dropouts (among whom over 60 percent now spend some time in prison). The corresponding estimates for black male high school graduates are 3.2 percent, 2.8 percentage points and 0.6 percentage points.

[79] Borjas et al. assume a stable demand function over a 40-year period. They allow for only a limited number of shifts by education or experience but otherwise assume constant employment responses to wage changes over time and across groups. In a period where labor demand has shifted so dramatically against less educated groups, it is very possible that some effects of demand shifts are attributed in this work to immigrant-induced labor supply shifts. Also, capital inflows in the long run are expected to fully offset the higher supplies of immigrant labor on average, thereby also dampening any negative effects for particular groups. See Ottavania and Peri (2006).

[80] Reed and Danziger estimate that immigration over the 1990s reduced the employment of black males with or without high school degrees by roughly one percentage point, and reduced their wages by 3.5 percent. Smith estimates that immigration over the past 15 years might have reduced teen employment rates by 5 percentage points overall, and about 4 points for blacks, but these effects diminish very quickly for young people over age 20.

differences across metropolitan areas (by Prof. David Card of Berkeley and others) have traditionally found much weaker evidence of negative impacts of immigration.

- Other evidence, including that by ethnographers, indicates that employers filling low-wage jobs requiring little reading/writing or communication clearly prefer immigrants to native-born blacks, and encourage informal networks through which immigrants gain better access to these jobs. The native-born black workers likely would be interested in some, but not all of these jobs, depending on their wages.

The ethnographic work (Moss and Tilly, 2001; Kirschenman and Neckerman, 1991) shows that employers perceive stronger work ethic among the immigrants, and a greater willingness to tolerate low wages. They use networks to encourage a ready flow of applicants from the friends and relatives of their immigrant workers. Some of these perceptions and the hiring behavior they generate might well reflect discrimination, especially against black men whom employers generally fear; some of it also likely reflects real differences in the attitudes and behaviors of workers from different groups, on average.[81]

As for the workers themselves, their interest will likely vary across the wages paid and sectors of the economy in which these jobs are found. I am inclined to believe that many black men would be interested in the residential construction or transportation jobs often filled by immigrants, but somewhat less interested in the low-wage agricultural or service jobs. Of course, in the absence of immigrants, these wages would rise somewhat. But whether they would rise sufficiently to induce a greater supply of black labor is questionable.[82]

- Our evidence does not allow us to distinguish the effects of legal v. illegal immigration on black Americans, though we can speculate about these differences to some extent.

On the one hand, illegal immigrants will often be paid sub-market wages, so the competition they generate will be even more intense for native-born workers; while their willingness to accept poor working conditions is greater than that of legal immigrants. On the other hand, the extent of their relative presence in the sectors where native-born blacks might really be interested in employment is unclear.

- The fact that the impacts of immigration are modest suggests that other factors are much more responsible for the negative trends in employment of black men and their

---

[81] Survey data in Holzer (1996) on application and hiring rates by race confirm that employers generally prefer Hispanic (including immigrant) applicants to those of blacks, while Holzer (1987) shows some of the difficulties blacks have using informal networks to gain employment. Falcon and Melendez (2001) also show that Hispanics use informal networks very effectively, though the jobs generated pay quite low wages. Evidence of continuing discrimination against black men in hiring clearly appears in the tester studies conducted by Pager (2003), while employer fears of this group are well-documented by Kirschenman and Neckerman *op. cit.*

[82] Evidence on the "reservation wages" (or minimally necessary wages for accepting employment) of young blacks relative to those of whites appears in Holzer (1986), while ethnographic data on the occupational perceptions and preferences of young black men appears in Young (2003). Lewis (2006) shows that employers who face fewer immigrants frequently use more capital-intensive production techniques, at least within manufacturing industries, rather than creating many higher-wage jobs. Thus, many such jobs would disappear in the absence of immigration before reaching the wages that might induce young blacks and other native-born workers to accept them.

rising incarceration rates, and therefore that other policies besides immigration reform might be needed to change these trends.

Interestingly, we might expect black women to have suffered as much from the influx of immigrants as did black men; yet the employment rates of low-income black women improved dramatically in the 1990s, as a result of welfare reform and the expansion of financial supports for the working poor (like the Earned Income Tax Credit and child support subsidies).[83]

Likewise, other forces are likely much more responsible for the decline in employment outcomes of black men and their rising incarceration rates. These include: 1) The declining availability of good-paying jobs to less-educated (and lower achieving) male workers, especially outside of the service sector; 2) The rising returns to illegal work, especially in the "crack" trade, in the 1980s; 3) The growing numbers of young blacks growing up in single-parent families and in poor neighborhoods; 4) Changes in attitudes and behavioral norms, on issues like schooling, employment and marriage; 5) Criminal justice policies that resulted in dramatically higher incarceration rates for those in the drug trade; and 6) Changes in child support enforcement that resulted in many default orders being set and many young men going into "arrears" on their payments.[84]

Accordingly, it is unlikely that any changes in immigration law will dramatically improve employment opportunities and outcomes for young blacks. To the extent that we "reform" immigration, we would want to carefully consider the full range of benefits that accrue to our economy and society from immigration, as well as its costs.[85] But, when considering how to improve outcomes of young blacks, we should instead focus mostly on:

1. Improving educational outcomes and achievement, starting with pre-kindergarten programs and continuing into higher education;

2. Enhancing youth development opportunities and mentoring for adolescents;

3. Improving their early work experience and occupational training with high-quality career and technical education;

4. Reducing incarceration rates (without increasing crime) and also the barriers to work faced by ex-offenders;

5. Extending the EITC to childless adults, including non-custodial fathers; and

6. Reforming child support regulations and taxes on "arrears" to encourage more labor force participation by non-custodial fathers.

---

[83] *See* Blank (2002).

[84] *See* Edelman *et al.* (2006) and Holzer *et al.* (2005) for more evidence and discussion of these issues.

[85] The benefits include lower prices for important consumer commodities, like food and housing, that are heavily used by lower-income families; these lower prices help raise their real incomes and offset the lower wages that might be generated by competition with immigrants. The provision of health care and elder care, which frequently suffer from worker shortages, is likely enhanced by immigration as well.

References

Blank, Rebecca. 2002. "Evaluating Welfare Reform in the United States." *Journal of Economic Literature*. 40:4, 1105-66.

Borjas, George; Jeffrey Grogger and Gordon Hanson. 2006. "Immigration and African-American Employment Opportunities: The Response of Wages, Employment and Incarceration to Labor Supply Shocks." National Bureau of Economic Research Working Paper No. 12518.

Edelman, Peter; Harry Holzer and Paul Offner. 2006. *Reconnecting Disadvantaged Young Men*. Washington DC: Urban Institute Press.

Falcon, Luis and Edwin Melendez. 2001. "The Social Context of Job Search for Racial Groups in Urban Centers." In L. Bobo *et al.* eds. Urban Inequality: Evidence from Four Cities. New York: Russell Sage Foundation.

Holzer, Harry J. 1987. "Informal Job Search and Black Youth Unemployment." *American Economic Review*. 77:2.

Holzer, Harry J. 1986. "Reservation Wages and their Labor Market Effects for Young White and Black Males." *Journal of Human Resources*. 21:2.

Holzer, Harry J. 1996. *What Employers Want: Job Prospects for Less-Educated Workers*. New York: Russell Sage Foundation.

Holzer, Harry; Paul Offner and Elaine Sorensen. 2005. "Declining Employment among Young Black Men: The Role of Incarceration and Child Support." *Journal of Policy Analysis and Management*. 24:2.

Kischenman, Joleen and Kathryn Neckerman. 1991. "We'd Love to Hire Them But..." In C. Jencks and P. Peterson eds. *The Urban Underclass*. Washington DC: Brookings Institution.

Lewis, Ethan. 2005. "Immigration, Skill Mix and the Choice of Technique." Federal Reserve Bank of Philadelphia Working Paper.

Moss, Philip and Chris Tilly. 2001. *Stories Employers Tell*. New York: Russell Sage Foundation.

Ottaviano, Gianmarco and Giovanni Peri. 2006. "Rethinking the Effects of Immigration on Wages." NBER Working Paper No. 12497.

Pager, Devah. 2003. "The Mark of a Criminal Record." *American Journal of Sociology*.

Reed, Deborah and Sheldon Danziger. 2007. "The Effects of Recent Immigration on Racial/Ethnic Labor Market Differences." *American Economic Review*. 97:2.

Smith, Christopher. 2008. "Dude, Where's My Job? The Impact of Immigration on the Youth Labor Market." Unpublished Ph.D. dissertation, Department of Economics, Massachusetts Institute of Technology.

Young, Alford. 2003. *The Minds of Marginalized Black Men*. Princeton University Press.

Julie Hotchkiss

Research Economist and Policy Advisor, Federal Reserve Bank of Atlanta

The Labor Market Experience and Impact of Undocumented Workers
(Version: March 28, 2008) by Julie L. Hotchkiss, Ph.D. and Myriam Quispe-Agnoli, Ph.D.

I. Introduction and Disclaimer

Thank you Mr. Chairman; I appreciate the opportunity to share with you and your fellow Commissioners the results of recent research I have undertaken with my colleague, Myriam Quispe-Agnoli, who is also here in the audience, on the issue of the impact and experience of undocumented workers here in the United States.

Before I begin, let me stress that the statements I make today are my own and do not represent the opinions or policy of the Federal Reserve Bank of Atlanta, or of the Federal Reserve System. Further, the motivation for undertaking this research was to inform the policy discussion, not to make specific policy recommendations.

II. Questions of the Analysis

A. How are wages impacted when the concentration of undocumented workers increases?

B. Is there any evidence of displacement of documented workers from firms that hire a greater share of undocumented workers?

C. Would we expect any greater downward pressure on wages in response to the presence of undocumented workers than in response to the presence legal immigrants?

III. Structure of the Statistical Analysis and Caveats

While I'm sure you'd rather I get straight to the answers to the questions I just listed, it's important to make sure that you are aware of some of the caveats and limitations of the research. All statistical analysis is limited by the data available, statistical tools at hand, and, I must admit, the imagination of the researcher.

The analysis is performed with information on workers and firms in the state of Georgia only. This research was possible as a result of a data sharing agreement that allowed me to have access to the Georgia Department of Labor administrative records used for administering the Unemployment Insurance program. These data are highly confidential and restricted in their access.

While analysis using data from only one state may seem limiting, Georgia was determined by one study to have experienced the fastest growth in its undocumented population between 2000 and 2006.[86] In addition, Georgia is ranked as sixth in the nation for size of

---

[86] U.S. Department of Homeland Security, Office of Immigration Statistics (August 2007), estimates 123% growth.

undocumented immigrant population.[87] So if this issue has relevance anywhere, certainly Georgia would be one of those places. It may also be particularly relevant for this hearing to note that 30 percent of the population in Georgia identifies itself as black or African American, ranking the state 4th in the U.S.[88] The implication is that a significant portion of the potentially impacted workforce in Georgia is black.

The data that we use contains quarterly earnings and SSNs on approximately 97 percent of all non-farm workers. We do not have information on workers' education, immigration status, or hours of work. We attempt to make up for limited worker information by repeating the analysis by sector, where we might find workers who are more alike than across sector. In addition, we account for the firm characteristics and any variation in wages that might be specific to the sector in which the worker is employed.

We identify undocumented workers by determining whether a worker's SSN is invalid. We use a simple algorithm based only on the value of the first three digits. This figure shows the share of workers in each of these broad industries that are identified as undocumented.

Figure 3. Percent of workers with invalid area numbers by broad industry, 1990:1 - 2006:4

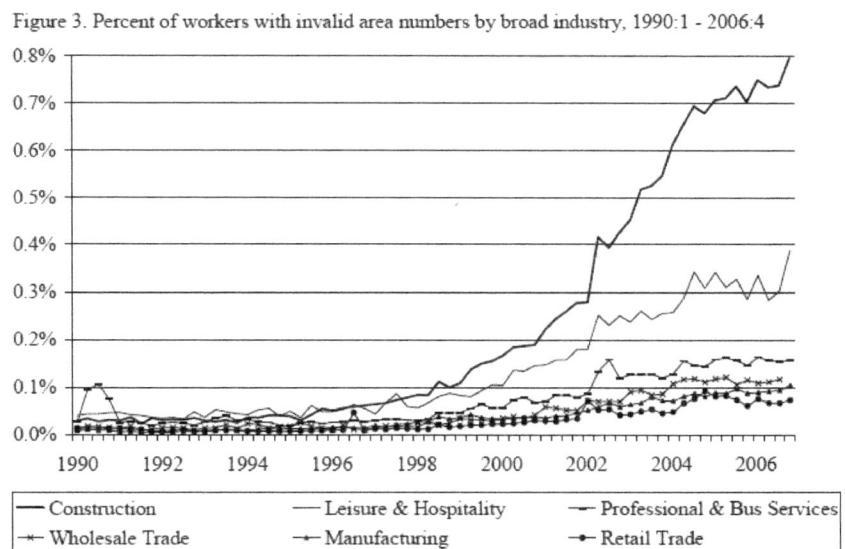

The first thing to note from this figure is that the growth in the share of undocumented workers is greatest in those sectors we might expect—construction; leisure and hospitality; and professional and business services, which includes landscaping services.

The second notable feature is that even in construction, the share of undocumented workers in our sample has reached a maximum of less than 1 percent of all workers in that sector. We are clearly undercounting the presence of undocumented workers in Georgia. The most recent estimate suggests that 7 percent of workers in Georgia are undocumented.[89] The

---

[87] Center for Immigration Studies (November 2007).

[88] American Community Survey (2006).

[89] Center for Immigration Studies (November 2007).

implication is that we are capturing only about two percent of all undocumented workers in the state, and, perhaps more importantly, this means that any impact of the presence of undocumented workers that we identify is expected to be an underestimate of the impact we would measure if we were capturing all undocumented workers in the analysis.

IV. Main Findings

A. Impact on Wages

Based on the most recent estimates of the growth of undocumented workers between 2000 and 2007, the share of undocumented workers in Georgia has increased from four to seven percent. Our analysis indicates that as a result of this growth in the share of undocumented workers, the annual earnings of the average documented worker in Georgia in 2007 were 2.9 percent ($960) lower than they were in 2000. The results for the construction industry were not very precise, but annual earnings for the average documented worker in the leisure and hospitality sector in 2007 were 9.1 percent ($1,520) lower than they were in 2000. This impact is expected to be lower for the U.S. overall, where we've seen only a two percentage point increase in undocumented workers.

In addition, these estimated impacts of the presence of undocumented workers on wages are larger than what others have found for the impact of immigrants as a whole.

B. Displacement

Our results show that an increase in the share of a firm's new hires that is undocumented leads to a *decrease* in documented workers leaving their jobs, but to an increase in undocumented worker leaving. Like others have found for immigrants overall, we find that newly arriving undocumented workers seems to displace earlier arriving undocumented workers, but have no adverse effect on the separation of documented workers.

How could it be that arrival of a new set of workers results in less separation? There are two mechanisms that could be at work to explain this—we did not test these theories, but offer them, as others have, to illustrate how this result can be consistent with economic theory.

When an input to the production process becomes less expensive, it should have two effects. In this case, it is labor that has become relatively less expensive with the arrival of undocumented workers. The first effect is what is called the *substitution effect*. The lower cost of labor entices firms to substitute away from capital inputs and use more labor; this increases the demand for labor, thus employment.

The second effect is called the *scale effect*. The idea here is that if one input to the production process becomes less expensive, total production becomes less expensive, inducing firms to increase production, which, in turn, increases demand for all inputs, including labor.

C. Why the impact of undocumented workers is expected to be greater

When workers do not have many alternative job prospects, they have been found to be less sensitive to wage changes than if they could find new employment easily. What this means is that these limited workers will be less likely to quit their jobs when they face low wages or hostile work environments. Historically, economists have found that married women, blacks, and workers with chronic medical conditions have behaved in this way.

When a worker finds himself in a limited employment situation, the worker acts as if the employer is the only one in town. The firm takes advantage of this position by paying lower wages. In fact, it's likely that labor market limitations are even greater for undocumented workers than for immigrants as a whole. This would provide an explanation for why the downward pressure on wages is even greater in the presence of undocumented workers than it is merely in the presence of immigrants.

The results of our third analysis indicate that undocumented workers are only about half as likely as documented workers to leave their jobs in response to a lower wage. This implies that it is the limited employment and grievance opportunities of undocumented workers that provide the likely mechanism through which their presence lowers wages.

V. Conclusions

Again, I am not here to promote or comment on any specific policy. However, the results from our research lead to three conclusions that we hope will be useful for the policy discussion:

- Wages will be higher in the absence of undocumented workers.

- Employment will not necessarily be higher, and may even be lower, in the absence of undocumented workers.

- And, any effective policy that reduces or eliminates workers' limited employment and grievance opportunities (which would include somehow legitimizing undocumented workers) will lead to higher wages for all workers, on average.

Thank you for your attention.

Steven A. Camarota

Immigration and Black Americans: Accessing the Impact

The issue of the impact of immigration on black Americans has long been debated. During the previous great wave of immigration at the turn of the last century, most black leaders such as D.W. Dubois, Booker T. Washington and A. Phillip Randolph felt that immigration harmed their community. Job competition has traditionally been the key issue, but other concerns exist as well. For example, the strain illegal immigration may create on public services may be particularly problematic for African Americans because, in many cases, schools and hospitals in some black areas are already stressed. Illegal immigration may add to this problem. There is also concern that by increasing demand, illegal immigration may drive up costs for low-income rental housing. When it comes to possible job competition, there are a number of areas of debate, but there are several areas on which there is general agreement. These areas of agreement are important because they should help frame the debate.

I will start my discussion with three areas on which there is general agreement. I will then move on to areas on which there is less agreement.

Three Areas of Agreement

First, there is little debate that illegal immigration primarily, though not exclusively, increases the supply of workers at the bottom end of the labor market. Occupational categories such as building cleaning and maintenance, food service and preparation, and construction are the most heavily impacted (See Table 1). If illegal immigration has a negative impact on U.S.-born workers, it will tend to be on those who have the least education because this is the kind of worker who generally does this type of job.

Second, all of the available data show that black men are disproportionately employed at the bottom end of the labor market. Compared to white men, a much larger share of native-born black men have relatively little education. About six out of 10 adult black men have only a high school degree or failed to graduate high school, compared to about four out of 10 white men (see Figure 1). I have estimated, as shown in Table 1, that about half (47 percent) of black men are employed in occupational categories that could be described as illegal-immigrant heavy. And unemployment among black men averages 13 percent in these same occupations. In contrast, only 34 percent of native-born white men are employed in occupations that have a heavy concentration of illegal immigrants; unemployment for white men averages 7 percent.

Third, there is a large body of research showing that less-educated black men, like less-educated workers overall, have generally not fared well in the U.S. labor market in recent years. This is true whether we look at wages, benefits, or labor force attachment. Workers with less than a high school education or those with only a high school education have seen wages decline or stagnate. The share of these workers offered benefits like health insurance by their employers has also declined. And while employment is cyclical, there has been a long-term trend of declining employment and labor force participation for less-educated native-born men, including less-educated black men.[90]

The overall deterioration in employment rates, wages, and benefits is a strong indication that less-educated labor is not in short supply. If such workers were in short supply, wages and benefits and employment rates would all be rising, as employers try desperately to attract and retain the relatively few workers available. But this seems to be exactly the opposite of what has been happening. The deterioration in the labor market for less-educated black men is particularly problematic because they already tended to make the lowest wages and have the lowest labor force participation rates.

There may be many possible explanations for the problems experienced by less-educated workers. But anyone asserting that labor is in short supply must directly address the declining wages and benefits. For example, if one argues that trade is a key reason for the decline, then it still means that access to foreign labor, through trade, is increasing the effective supply of labor in the United States and exerting downward pressure on wages. If one argues that technological innovation is increasing productivity, which may also increase the effective supply of workers as well as reduce demand for less-skilled workers, then once again the supply of workers is being increased, and this undermines the idea that workers are scarce. Any assertion that less-skilled workers are very scarce must address the overwhelming economic evidence in wages, benefits, and employment to the contrary. Testimonials from employers, who understandably wish to keep wages low, are not systematic evidence.

The Impact of Immigration on Black Workers

Several studies have found that immigration has impacted the wages or employment of native-born African Americans. This includes recent studies by Borjas, Grogger, and Hanson that found that immigration reduces labor force participation of the least-educated black men.[91] Research by Andrew Sum, Paul Harrington, and Ishwar Khatiwada at Northeastern University has found that immigrants are displacing young native-born men in the labor market and that the largest impact is on blacks and Hispanics.[92] In my own research I have found that blacks are more likely to be in competition with immigrants than are whites.[93] A 1995 study by Augustine Kposowa concluded that, "non-whites appear to

---

[90] See for example, *The State of Working America*, 2006/07 by Lawrence Mishel, Jared Bernstein, and Sylvia Allegretto.

[91] *Immigration and African-American Employment Opportunities: The Response of Wages, Employment, and Incarceration to Labor Supply Shocks.* By George J. Borjas, Jeffrey Grogger, and Gordon H. Hanson Working Paper 12518.

[92] *The Impact of New Immigrants on Young Native-Born Workers, 2000-2005,* September 2006 By Andrew Sum, Paul Harrington, and Ishwar Khatiwada.

[93] In addition to the results shown in Table 1, which focus on illegal immigration, in a 1998 study published by the Center for Immigration Studies, I found that native-born blacks are more likely to be in competition with immigrants than are whites. *The Wages of Immigration: The Effect on the Low-Skilled Labor Market.*

lose jobs to immigrants and their earnings are depressed by immigrants."[94] A 1998 study of the New York area by Howell and Mueller found that a 10 percentage point increase in the immigrant share of an occupation reduced wages of black men about five percentage points. Given the large immigrant share of the occupations they studied, this implies a significant impact on native-born blacks.[95]

There certainly is a good deal of anecdotal evidence that employers often prefer immigrants, particularly Hispanic and Asian immigrants, over native-born black Americans. A more qualitative study by anthropologist Katherine Newman and Chauncy Lennon of fast food jobs in Harlem, found that immigrants are much more likely to get hired than are native-born black Americans.[96]

Some studies have not found an impact on blacks from immigration. Most studies that have found little or no impact are based on comparisons of labor market outcomes across cities with different levels of immigrants. Part of the reason it is hard to estimate the effect of immigration in this way is that we live in a national economy. The movement of capital, labor, goods, and services tends to create wage and employment equilibrium between American cities. Moreover, immigrants are attracted to cities with higher wage and employment growth. This will tend to mask the impact of immigration. As a result, comparisons across cities will tend to understate the immigration effect. Studies that have tended to treat the country as one large labor market have found larger effects than have cross city comparisons.

Conclusion

There is no debate that illegal immigration, and even immigration more generally, increases the supply of workers who are employed in lower-skilled, lower-wage sectors of the economy. It is also uncontested that a significant share of native-born black men have education levels that make them more likely to compete with illegal immigrants. Additionally, there is agreement that wages and employment for less-educated men, including black men, have generally stagnated or declined. The lack of wage growth makes it very difficult to argue that less-educated workers are in short supply. There are a number of studies indicating that immigration is harming the labor market prospects of black Americans. However, the debate over whether immigration reduces wages or employment among black Americans is not entirely settled. If one is concerned about less-educated workers in this country, it is difficult to justify continuing high levels of legal and illegal immigration that disproportionately impact the bottom end of the labor market.

---

[94] Augustine J. Kposowa, "The Impact of Immigration on Unemployment and Earnings among Racial Minorities in the United States," in *Ethnic and Racial Studies,* Volume 18, Number 3, July 1995.

[95] "The Effects of Immigrants on African-American Earnings: A Jobs-Level Analysis of the New York City Labor Market, 1979-89" (November 1997). Levy Economics Institute Working Paper No. 210. By David Howell and Elizabeth Mueller.

[96] "Finding Work in the Inner City: How Hard Is it Now? How Hard Will it Be for AFDC Recipients?" by Katherine Newman and Chauncy Lennon.

It is important to understand that immigration does not simply reduce wages or employment. There is a good deal of agreement among economists that the benefit to more-educated natives that comes from reducing the wages of the least-educated Americans must be very small. A 1997 study by the National Research Council, *The New Americans,* has a good explanation as to why the gains are so small. There is no body of research showing large economic gains to native-born Americans from immigration. The primary beneficiary of immigration seems to be the immigrants themselves. A central part of the immigration debate is how we weight the benefits that go to immigrants against the losses suffered by the poorest and least-educated Americans. How one answers this question will have a significant impact on what immigration policy makes the most sense.

Table 1

Characteristics by Occupational Category									
All Figures Are for Men 16 and Older									
	Occupation	Illegal share (est.)	Total immigrant share (legal & illegal)	Share of occup. comprised of native-born blacks	Share of occup. comprised of native-born whites	Share of all native-born blacks who are employed in occup.	Native-born black unemp rate	Share of all native-born whites who are employed in occup.	Native-born white unemp rate
Highest Illegal Occup.	Farming, fishing & forestry	22%	36%	5%	53%	1%	10%	1%	7%
	Construct. & extraction	18%	30%	5%	56%	8%	19%	10%	9%
	Blding cleaning & maintenance	15%	32%	13%	46%	6%	12%	3%	10%
	Food service & preparation	14%	29%	9%	50%	5%	17%	3%	7%
	Production	8%	19%	9%	63%	10%	8%	8%	5%
	Transportation & moving	6%	17%	14%	58%	17%	9%	8%	7%
Lowest Illegal Occup.	Installlation & repair	4%	14%	6%	70%	5%	8%	7%	3%
	Healthcare support	3%	22%	15%	48%	1%	2%	0%	4%
	Computer mathematical	3%	23%	4%	65%	2%	4%	3%	2%
	Office & admin. Support	3%	13%	13%	60%	11%	9%	6%	5%
	Arts, entertain. & media	2%	12%	5%	74%	1%	8%	2%	5%
	Personal care & service	2%	18%	11%	58%	2%	9%	1%	6%
	Sales	2%	12%	6%	72%	9%	7%	12%	3%
	Life, phy. & soc. science	2%	21%	3%	65%	0%	4%	1%	1%
	Education, training	2%	12%	6%	74%	2%	6%	3%	1%
	Architecture & engineering	1%	15%	3%	74%	1%	4%	4%	1%
	Management occp.	1%	11%	4%	78%	6%	4%	15%	2%
	Protective service	1%	6%	14%	70%	5%	4%	3%	3%
	Healthcare practitioner	1%	18%	7%	68%	2%	7%	3%	1%
	Business & financial	1%	12%	6%	75%	3%	4%	4%	2%
	Community & social service	1%	9%	17%	65%	2%	7%	1%	1%
	legal occp.	0%	4%	3%	86%	0%	0%	1%	2%
	Total Labor Force	6%	18%	8%	65%	100%	10%	4%	100%

Source: Center for Immigration Studies analysis of the March 2007 Current Population Survey. Figures for native-born black and white men are for those 16 years of age and older who are non-Hispanic and chose only one race.

Figure 1

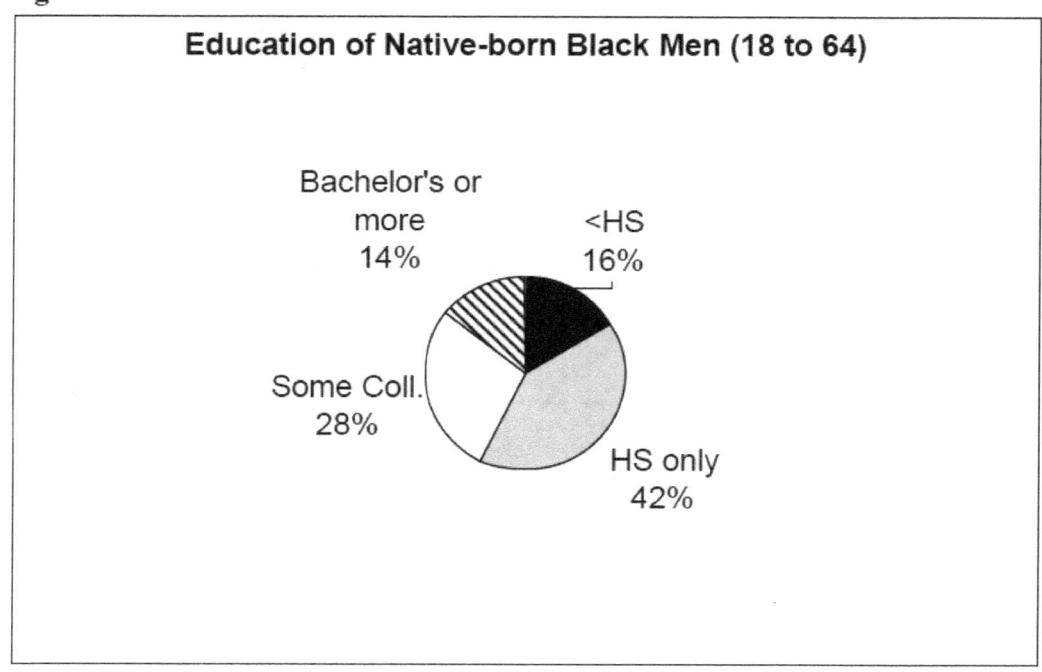

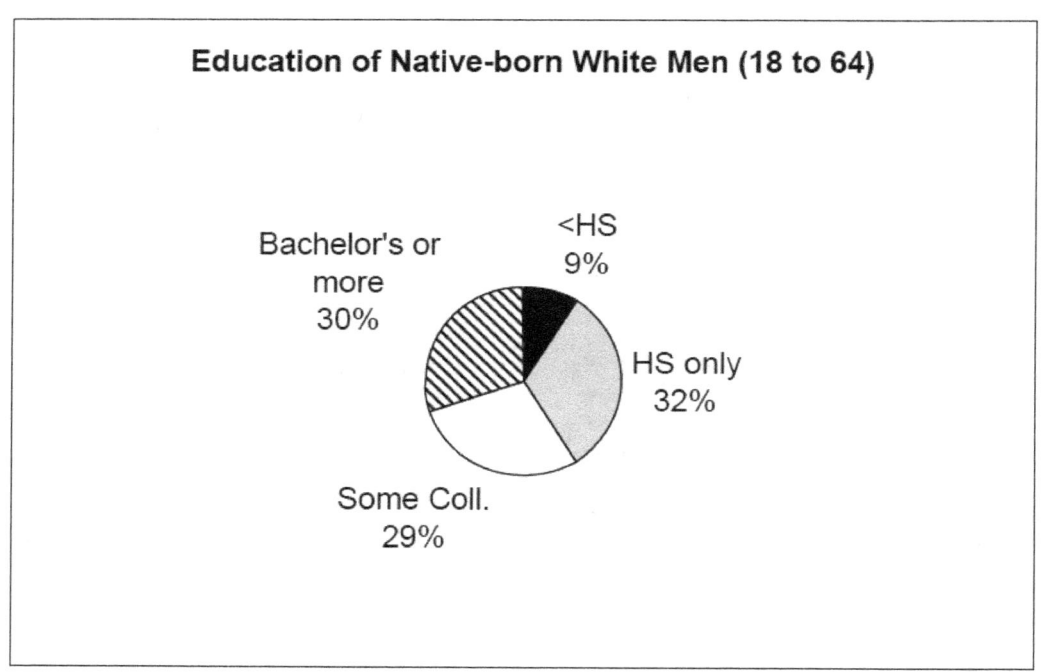

Richard Nadler

The Impact of Immigration, Legal and Illegal, on the Employment Status of Black Workers and the Poverty Status of African American Children

Ladies and gentlemen, members of the Commission: I'm honored by your invitation to be here today, to cast such modicum of light as I can on what has become a potentially explosive social issue. I'm speaking of the impact of mass immigration, roughly three-quarters of it Hispanic, on the economic plight of African Americans.

During the first decade of the new century, the immigrant population of the United States has increased by a million residents per year on net, half of them illegal. This inflow, roughly 3.5 immigrants per 1,000 residents annually, exceeds the normative rate of the past century by little. But a great debate rages regarding its consequences.

Critics call it an invasion.

A recent ad campaign, sponsored by the Coalition for the Future American Worker, features Dr. Frank Morris, the former executive director of the Congressional Black Caucus Foundation. In it, Dr. Morris says, quote: "Immigration accounts for 40 percent of the decline in employment of African American men."

In another spot, he tells his viewers, quote: "If you're a Black American, you've noticed many of us are out of work. You've probably also noticed the huge increase in immigration. Those two facts are related."

Many are the woes attributed to immigration in general, and to illegal immigration in particular: downward pressure on wages and innovation, and upward pressures on unemployment, poverty and crime. Many are the remedies proposed to these problems, ranging from skills-testing to mass deportations.

Immigrations critics of the Left and Right present differing and conflicting analyses of the impact of contemporary immigration. The conservative critics believe that the free movement of labor is generally beneficial, but that particular characteristics of the current wave negate these benefits. Some contend that the low skill level of illegal immigrants retards innovation, or capitalization per worker. Others say that the cultural mismatch of the Latin American poor to contemporary American life imposes tax costs that outweigh benefits.

On the Left, critics regard contemporary immigration as an oversupply of labor, particularly in low-skill jobs, driving unemployment and crime up, and wages down, particularly among the urban poor.

But on one thing the immigration critics, Left and Right, agree: the market model of Laissez Faire has broken down, at least as regards the world's "tired, poor and huddled masses, yearning to be free."

But has it really? As I listened to the unfolding debate over comprehensive immigration reform, it struck me that the assertions of critics were widely credited as fact; indeed, that the threshold question was seldom raised, let alone answered.

Do high levels of immigration correlate to high levels of the various ills attributed to it? My own work in this field, "Immigration and the Wealth of States," matched the immigration patterns of the 50 states and the District of Columbia to data that immigration ostensibly affected—Gross State Product, Personal Income, Disposable Income, Median Income (household and per capita); rates of poverty and unemployment; and rates of crime. The study focused particularly on recent trends, state-by-state, 2000 to 2007.

The critics of immigration are not always consistent in what they mean by it. In disaggregating high-immigrations jurisdictions (states + the District of Columbia), I used all three definitions suggested by the Center for Immigration Studies' Steven Camarota in his paper, "Immigrants in the United States, 2007: A Profile of America's Foreign-Born Population" (CIS, Nov. 2007).

The "high percentage" jurisdictions [> (%)] in my study were the 10 states (including DC) with the highest proportion of immigrants in their resident population. This is a useful definition, but it does not differentiate between settled immigrants and recent arrivals.

The "high influx" states [> (+)] were the 10 whose population in 2007 was most altered, percentage-wise, by an influx of immigrants since 2000. This set captures a considerable percentage of the least settled and most mobile immigrants. At least half of the immigration since 2000 has been illegal.

The "high number" [> (#)] states were the 10 states with the most foreign-born individuals, regardless of percentages. This definition includes one state with many immigrants not captured in the other two: Illinois.

These three overlapping groups of 10 encompassed 19 separate jurisdictions containing 82.6 percent of the U.S. immigrant population and 60.4 percent of the nation's African American population.

In what follows, I will speak of these 19 as the high immigration jurisdictions—HIJs—and the other 32 states, where 17.4 percent of the immigrant population resides, as "low-immigration." The study, which the commission staff has made available to you, lists the states in each immigration subgroup.

Were it true that high immigration correlated with a slow-down in capitalization per worker, this should be reflected in Gross State Product trends. It was not. The HIJs—high immigration jurisdictions—experienced Gross State Product growth significantly higher than the other 32 states.

Were it true that high immigration decreased income in its broadest measure, then the states with low immigration should have an advantage in personal income per capita. But in fact, personal income per capita was not only higher in the HIJs, but was increasing at a significantly faster rate.

Were it true that the costs associated with high levels of immigration negated its benefits, then that should be reflected in state statistics on disposable income—after-tax income. But in fact, the HIJs had a significant advantage over low immigration states in disposable income and disposable income per capita, whether measured in dollar amounts or in rates of increase.

"Median income" defines the center of a set of earners—the income point at which half earn more, and half earn less. If contemporary immigration constitutes a "war against the middle class," as Lou Dobbs contends, then median incomes should be declining in HIJs, either absolutely, or at least in relation to other states.

The opposite is true. Median income, whether household or individual, whether measured in dollars or by trend-over-time, fared better in the high immigration jurisdictions than in the rest of the country. This advantage held true not only for the 19 HIJs together, but for the three component subgroups separately.

No matter how you slice it or dice it, the HIJs have outperformed the 32 low immigration states economically. But what of the social costs? In 2006, unemployment was 4.6 percent nationally. In the HIJs, it was lower than average—4.4 percent in the full set, and 4.2 percent in the rapid influx subset—the group with the highest likely influx of illegals from 2000 to 2007. Unemployment in the low immigrations states was 4.9 percent.

Twelve and seven-tenths percent (12.7%) of U.S. households earned annual income below the federally defined poverty line in 2006, compared to 12.0 percent in the 19 HIJs, and 10.3 percent in the "rapid influx" subset. In the 32 low immigration states, the household poverty level stood at 13.7 percent—a percent above the national average.

The F.B.I. unified crime reports define crime rate as crimes committed per 100,000 residents. In 2006, the HIJs had a crime rate of 3,807 per 100,000 residents compared to 3,809 in the low-immigration states. In other words, the crime rates were virtually identical.

To summarize: high state levels of immigration, variously defined, correlate with above average performance in Gross State Product, Personal Income, Disposable Income, and Median Income, and below average rates of Individual and Household Poverty and Unemployment. This may not be what you're hearing on Fox News or CNN. But it happens to be true.

Now none of these findings relates directly to the impact of contemporary immigration on African Americans. But they raise some serious questions regarding assertions like those raised by Dr. Morris.

The states with 83 percent of the immigrant population contain 60 percent of the black population as well. If immigrants are themselves heavy users of welfare, and likelier-than-average to live in poverty, then why should HIJs have better-than-average rates of poverty and unemployment?

In preparation for this hearing, I developed additional charts that extend the methodology of "Immigration and the Wealth of States" to black unemployment and African American child poverty, state by state. Allow me to summarize them for you.

State Employment Data on Black Unemployment, by Immigration Set and Subset

Despite a steady immigrant flow during the current administration, black unemployment tracked general unemployment. It increased during the first three years of this administration, from 7.6 percent in 2000 to 10.8 percent in 2003, then decreased for the next four years to 8.3 percent in 2007. In both 2000 and 2007, black unemployment was 3.6 percent higher than the national rates of unemployment (4.0 percent in 2000, and 4.6 percent in 2007).

In other words, from 2000 to 2007, unemployment increased an identical 0.6 percent nationwide and among Blacks. But when we compare black employment trends in the HIJs and the low immigration states, a different picture emerges. (We note here that the American Community Survey, from which the numbers are taken, does not report separate black unemployment results for the high-immigration states of Hawaii and Utah because the sample sizes render the results insignificant.)

Af American Unemployment in the High Immigration Jurisdictions – 2000					
State	Bl Labor Force	Unemployed	No. of Immigrants 2000	% Black Unemployed	
US	16,603,000	1,269,000	27,022,000	7.6%	US
NY	1,386,000	110,000	3,228,000	7.9%	NY
GA	1,334,000	86,000	570,000	6.4%	GA
FL	1,067,000	67,000	2,385,000	6.3%	FL
TX	1,108,000	86,000	2,367,000	7.8%	TX
CA	1,086,000	82,000	9,053,000	7.6%	CA
MD	845,000	54,000	455,000	6.4%	MD
IL	900,000	99,000	1,211,000	11.0%	IL
VA	96,000	30,000	580,000	4.3%	VA
NJ	595,000	51,000	1,368,000	8.6%	NJ
MA	198,000	12,000	694,000	6.1%	MA
CT	201,000	8,000	309,000	4.0%	CT
DC	158,000	13,000	48,000	8.2%	DC
AZ	90,000	2,000	607,000	2.2%	AZ
WA	114,000	9,000	483,000	7.9%	WA
NV	58,000	4,000	352,000	6.9%	NV
DE	89,000	5,000	42,000	5.6%	DE
RI	26,000	2,000	119,000	7.7%	RI

Fifty-five percent of the African American labor force resides in nine high immigration states. In six of these (NY, FL, TX, MD, VA, & NJ), including three of the top four, the African American unemployment rate went *down* from 2000 to 2007:

Af Am Unemployment in the High Immigration Jurisdictions – 2007				
State	**Bl labor force**	**Unemployed**	**# of Immigrants 2007**	**% Bl Unemployed**	
US	17,496,000	1,445,000	37,280,000	8.3%	US
NY	1,488,000	113,000	4,105,000	7.6%	NY
GA	1,406,000	106,000	953,000	7.5%	GA
FL	1,350,000	82,000	3,453,000	6.1%	FL
TX	1,291,000	96,000	3,438,000	7.4%	TX
CA	1,068,000	103,000	9,980,000	9.6%	CA
MD	848,000	45,000	731,000	5.3%	MD
IL	842,000	90,000	1,702,000	10.7%	IL
VA	748,000	34,000	856,000	4.5%	VA
NJ	573,000	46,000	1,869,000	8.0%	NJ
MA	193,000	8,000	897,000	4.1%	MA
CT	183,000	16,000	443,000	8.7%	CT
DC	142,000	13,000	78,000	9.2%	DC
AZ	111,000	7,000	891,000	6.3%	AZ
WA	106,000	10,000	722,000	9.4%	WA
NV	95,000	6,000	457,000	6.3%	NV
DE	89,000	4,000	77,000	4.5%	DE
RI	35,000	2,000	140,000	5.7%	RI

Here is a summary chart of the movement in unemployment, by immigration group and sub-group:

Black Unemployment, 2000 & 2007			
2000		**2007**	
U.S.	7.6%	U.S.	8.3%
32 states low immigration	8.3%	32 states low immigration	9.6%
17 high immigration	7.2%	17 high immigration	7.4%
10 > (#)	7.4%	10 > (#)	7.6%
9 > (%)	7.4%	9 > (%)	7.5%
9 > (+)	6.2%	9 > (+)	6.1%

- Black unemployment went up three times as much in the U.S. as a whole as in the HIJs—0.6 percent vs. 0.2 percent

- Black unemployment went up six-and-a-half times as much in the low immigrations states as in the HIJs—1.3 percent vs. 0.2 percent

- The subgroup of states in which black unemployment actually decreased was the "high influx" subgroup—the jurisdictions where the immigrant inflow, 2000–2007 constituted *the highest percentage of state resident population.*

The above tables do not prove that high rates of immigration, taken as a single factor, cause enhanced rates of black employment. But critics of immigration must explain why black employment, both as a rate and as a trend, has been generally superior *at the points of immediate impact* than in places where no such immigration impact has occurred.

State Data on Child Poverty, by Immigration Set and Subset

Compiling household poverty data by race and state in the interim between one decennial census and the next is like painting a bull's eye on a moving target. The researcher must work from the Census Bureau's Current Population Survey Annual Social and Economic Supplements. The sample sizes, disaggregated in this way, may be quite small, so it is customary to merge a number of years into a rolling average. The dollar amount of the federal poverty level is adjusted year to year, requiring additional adjustments. The date of this hearing has not allowed me to do this, but the National Center for Children in Poverty at Columbia University has provided a useful analogue. They have calculated poverty numbers and rates for African American children, state-by-state. As explained at their website, http://www.nccp.org/profiles/US_profile_7.html:

> "State data were calculated from the Annual Social and Economic Supplement (the March supplement) of the Current Population Survey from 2005, 2006, and 2007, representing information from calendar years 2004, 2005, and 2006. NCCP averaged three years of data because of small sample sizes in less populated states. The national data were calculated from the 2007 data, representing information from the previous calendar year... Families and children are defined as poor if family income is below the federal poverty threshold. The poverty threshold for a family of four with two children was $21,200 in 2008, $20,650 in 2007, and $20,000 in 2006."

The NCCP numbers exclude children of ethnic Latinos who report their race as black, and children who were reported as "more than one race."

The NCCP numbers also exclude those states that, even with a three year spread, yield sample sizes too small for meaningful analysis.

As a result, 15 of our original 19 "high immigrations jurisdictions" remain, and only 19 of the 32 "low immigration states." Nonetheless, *the included states contain the overwhelming majority of the NCCP's estimate of Black children in poverty*—10,837,515 of 10,922,206. The chart below summarizes the findings:

African American Child Poverty, 2006 (est.) by Immigration Group & Subgroup				
	Total Black Children	**Black Children in poverty**	**Black non-poor children**	**% in poverty**
U.S. (Charted states only)	10,837,515	3,699,034	7,138,481	34%
19 low immigration	4,788,560	1,873,443	7,138,425	39%
15 high immigration	6,048,955	1,825,591	4,223,364	30%
9 (>) states	5,303,562	1,651,147	3,652,415	31%
8 (%) states	3,701,537	1,147,242	2,554,295	31%
8 (+) states	2,168,575	546,716	1,621,859	25%

- The African American child poverty rate in the 15 HIJs was 30 percent—4 percent lower than the national average, and 9 percent lower than the child poverty rate for the low-immigration states.

- All three of the high immigration subsets have black child poverty rates below both the "low immigration state" average and the national average.

- Among the immigration subsets, *the lowest black child poverty rate is found in the "rapid influx" group*—the states whose population has been most impacted, percentage-wise, by an inflow of immigrants since 2007.

The chart on the following page lists the NCCP calculations of African American children in poverty state-by-state, and the percentage of black children that this number represents. The shaded states are those that qualify under one or more of the definitions of "high-immigration states" used in "Immigration and the Wealth of States," Americas Majority Foundation, Jan. 2008. (See pages 14 and 15.)

Where the NCCP researchers conclude that a sample is too small to be meaningful, I have listed the state, but left its fields blank.

Now, "child poverty" is not identical to "household poverty." But it is no far stretch to recognize that the rates of African American child poverty are reflective of black household poverty. Again, those who believe that immigration, legal or illegal, is causative of black poverty have some explaining to do. If immigration were a primary factor, why would its effect be less where its signature is substantial? Or least where its *immediate* impact is greatest?

An easy answer is that "immigrants follow opportunity." But this begs the question. To a market economist, voluntary migration of labor is not merely an effect of prosperity, but a cause. The opportunity that the "poor, huddled masses yearning to breathe free" grasp in America reduces costs to consumers, and liberates capital for new investment. This in turn increases the demand for labor in other sectors, offsetting the initial loss of wages. Economic freedom is not a zero sum game.

African American Child Poverty, 2006 (est.)			
	Total Black Children	**Black children in poverty**	**Black Children Non-poor**	**% poverty**
U.S. (separately calculated)	10,600,965			34%
Alabama	346,131	145,375	200,756	42%
Alaska				
Arizona				
Arkansas	131,883	55,391	76,492	42%
California	649,241	188,280	460,961	29%
Colorado	330,063	99,019	231,044	30%
Connecticut	91,163	17,321	73,842	19%
Delaware	45,321	8,611	36,710	19%
Dist of Col	78,964	30,796	48,168	39%
Florida	845,814	245,286	600,528	29%
Georgia	784,964	259,038	525,926	33%
Hawaii				
Idaho				
Illinois	566,689	215,342	351,347	38%
Indiana	168,872	77,681	91,191	46%
Iowa	22,838	12,104	10,734	53%
Kansas	48,680	22,393	26,287	46%
Kentucky	95,736	37,337	58,399	39%
Louisiana	429,503	171,801	257,702	40%
Maine				
Maryland	453,335	90,667	362,668	20%
Massachusetts	156,903	61,192	95,711	39%
Michigan	432,251	177,223	255,028	41%
Minnesota	75,447	27,161	48,286	36%
Mississippi	330,968	155,555	175,413	47%
Missouri	200,503	78,196	122,307	39%
Montana				
Nebraska				
Nevada	58,931	21,215	37,716	36%
New Hampshire				
New Jersey	328,916	62,494	266,422	19%
New Mexico				
New York	787,325	283,437	503,888	36%
North Carolina	541,297	189,454	351,843	35%
North Dakota				
Ohio	405,357	190,518	214,839	47%
Oklahoma	85,084	32,332	52,752	38%
Oregon				
Pennsylvania	361,964	152,025	209,939	42%
Rhode Island	17,679	5,834	11,845	33%
South Carolina	354,252	95,648	258,604	27%
South Dakota				

(continued)	Total Black Children	Black children in poverty	Black Children Non-poor	% poverty
Tennessee	314,620	110,117	204,503	35%
Texas	795,444	254,542	540,902	32%
Utah				
Vermont				
Virginia	388,267	81,536	306,731	21%
Washington				
West Virginia				
Wisconsin	113,110	44,113	68,997	39%
Wyoming				
Totals:	**10,837,515**	**3,699,034**	**7,138,481**	**34%**

Now, classical economics does not claim that an increased supply of labor must at all times tend to the general welfare. Labor is only one element of production, and if other factors become less free, or more scarce, then a general contraction in living standards may follow. That, in fact, describes the preconditions for *emigration*—the reasons why people leave the country of their birth for a strange land.

But should such a general contraction occur in America—and our studies do not suggest that this has yet occurred—the optimal solution to an oversupply of labor would be a reduction of impediments to emigration. As things stand now, the undocumented—or if you prefer, illegal—immigrant has no practical path to legal work status, and powerful reasons to stay in America even if the work dries up.

This summer, when Congress rejected comprehensive immigration reform—an approach simultaneously recognizing the humanity of the immigrant worker, the claims of commerce, and public demand for border control—it robbed itself of the tools that could fine-tune either the market forces or the security interests that underlie the current debate.

But these matters lead us into policy areas broader than today's topic.

Carol M. Swain

Illegal Immigration and Black Unemployment

I would like to commend the U.S. Civil Rights Commission for its decision to investigate the impact of illegal immigration on the wages and employment prospects of low-income black Americans.

It is significant that the Civil Rights Commission chose to have this important discussion today on the 40th anniversary of the assassination of Martin Luther King Jr. in Memphis. It is significant because Dr. King was in Memphis to support black sanitation workers who were striking because of their poor working conditions, and today we come together to discuss new threats to black employment. In Dr. King's mountaintop speech the night before he was killed, he called for us to grapple with issues of injustice and fair treatment for all our citizens. I'm not sure whether Dr. King could have predicted that black Americans—now granted full status as citizens—would face threats to their ability to earn a living from non-citizens, from illegal immigrants. But I can say that although much has changed in 40 years, there are still mountains to climb.

National surveys show that white and black Americans are united in their calls for immigration reform.[97] Many of the problems and issues identified by researchers have a potentially negative impact on the social, political, and economic wellbeing of non-blacks as well.

It is crucial, therefore, that we note this when we discuss the impact of immigration on black America. Otherwise, we risk the dismissal of our findings as attributable to deficiencies inherent in blacks themselves rather than to larger institutional and systemic forces that work against the interests of a much wider population.

I am the editor of *Debating Immigration*, an anthology published last year by Cambridge University Press. My comments today will be focused primarily on black unemployment and some of the factors that I believe account for the overrepresentation of blacks among the nation's unemployed.

Figure 1 presents unemployment rates by race and year from 1990 through 2006. It shows that black rates of unemployment are consistently higher than other groups. In June 2004 the overall unemployment rate was 5.6 percent with white unemployment at 5.0 percent, black unemployment at 10.2 percent, and Hispanic unemployment at 6.7 percent.

---

[97] Brian DeBose, "Blacks, Whites View Immigration Similarly, Poll Says Think U.S. should limit number," The Washington Post, November 17, 2005, A12; Jeff Diamond, "African American Attitudes Towards Immigration Policy," Internal Migration Review 32, No.2 (Summer 1998): 451-470; Gallup Poll News Service, "Gallup Poll Social Series Governance," Field survey (09/12/2005-09/15/2005), Qn42.

By June 2005 the economy as a whole seemed to be improving. The overall unemployment rate dropped to 5.0 percent. However, the employment situation for blacks did not improve. In fact, black unemployment actually increased to 10.3 percent, up from 10.2 percent the previous year.

So, while white unemployment dropped from 5.0 percent to 4.3 percent and Hispanic unemployment dropped from 6.9 percent to 5.8 percent, blacks saw their unemployment rate increase.

Among the black unemployed are a disproportionate percentage of black high school dropouts and graduates. In fact, during the 2003 recession, blacks aged 16–24 were nearly two-and-a-half times more likely to be unemployed than white workers and, by a slight margin black graduates, constituting 40 percent of the black population, were more adversely affected than members of other groups. When job gains have occurred for blacks, it has been disproportionately in dead end, low sector jobs.

Declining wages adversely impact low skill workers. A study published by the Pew Hispanic Center in 2004 found significant employment gains for Hispanics in newly created low-wage jobs although these gains were offset by reduced earnings for the newer immigrants who were suffering a two-year decline in wages.[98]

What accounts for high rates of black unemployment?

A few possible causes include:

  a) An oversupply of low-skilled workers
  b) Racial discrimination by employers
  c) Inadequate education and training

Let's look at each of these more closely. Dr. Steven Camarota has argued that the high black and Hispanic unemployment rates can be partially attributed to the oversupply of low-skilled immigrants arriving since 1990. These newcomers have increased the supply of labor by 25 percent for the kinds of jobs traditionally taken by high school dropouts and graduates.[99] While immigrant workers constitute 15 percent of the U.S. labor force, they are a whopping 40 percent of workers without high school diplomas.[100] Only 12 percent have greater than a high school diploma.[101] As a consequence, the greatest competition occurs among people at the margins of society, a group that includes poorly educated blacks, whites, and Hispanics who compete against each other and against new immigrants for low-wage, low-skill jobs.

---

[98] Rakesh Kochbar, "Latino Labor Report, 2004: More Jobs for Immigrants but at Lower Wages," Report of the Pew Hispanic Center, 18.

[99] Steven A. Camarota, Testimony for U.S. House Committee on Education and the Workforce, November 16, 2005.

[100] Ibid.

[101] Ibid.

Continued racial discrimination in the labor market is a second documented factor that helps to explain black unemployment. Princeton University Professor Devah Pager has shown that some employers confronted with a black male job applicant with similar education, work history, style of presentation and clean criminal record, is less likely to get a call back than a white male applicant with a felony conviction.[102] Blacks with felony convictions were almost totally shut out of the labor market.

Inadequate education is another factor. Clearly, our primary and secondary educational system is failing to meet the needs of many ethnic minorities and working class whites. Cuts in state and federal programs have made it far more difficult for lower and working class students to get the preparation needed to prepare themselves for higher paying jobs and advanced educational opportunities.

Conclusion

Blacks are our nation's big losers and most undesired group. Few people seriously expect illegal immigrants to be returned home. When Congress gets around to legalizing the millions of illegal immigrants residing in the country, there will be even more increased competition for social welfare programs, educational opportunities, jobs, and low-income housing. If history repeats itself, black Americans will continue to be the nation's biggest losers.

Persistent black unemployment is not helped by the oversupply of labor or by the decisions of employers who prefer new immigrants and white ex-felons to blacks with no criminal offenses. Persistent and lingering discrimination fuels the anger and frustration that many blacks feel towards America, and it contributes to growing ethnic conflict and ethnic violence between blacks and Hispanics in urban neighborhoods.

Black unemployment is also a likely contributing factor to some of the dysfunctional conditions found in some black communities, such as high rates of violent crime, single parent households, illegitimacy, infant mortality, drug use, and infectious diseases. It doesn't have to be this way. We can positively impact a range of conditions just by helping to reduce black unemployment.

What should we do to reform immigration?

I believe that an independent commission akin to those used for military base closings will be needed to reform immigration. A reform package must restore confidence in the rule of law, make it costlier for employers to discriminate against native workers, and must increase penalties for anyone found in the country illegally. To assist native workers, we must invest in education, create incentives for employers to train and hire new workers, and create a tamperproof Social Security card. Such efforts would help protect and expand the gains of historically disadvantaged populations, including poor whites and legal immigrants.

---

[102] Devah Pager, *Marked: Race, Crime, and Finding Work in the Era of Mass Incarcerations.* Chicago: University of Chicago Press, 2007.

Public Comment

Mrs. Kimela Santifer-Berry of Los Angeles, in a letter to the Commission, wrote that the Commission's briefing was an acknowledgment that illegal immigration was a problem, and that in her view, her city was becoming a third-world country. She related that many workers in businesses and shops where she was a customer had non-English speaking staff, despite the English-language speaking clientele. She objected also to what she viewed as jobs for young people being filled by illegal workers, particularly jobs that she believed would otherwise be filled by African Americans. She invited the Commission to visit Los Angeles to draw their own conclusions, particularly in the African American communities with high unemployment.

Speaker Biographies

Gordon Hanson

Gordon H. Hanson is the Director of the Center on Pacific Economies and Professor of Economics at the University of California at San Diego, where he holds faculty positions in the Graduate School of International Relations and Pacific Studies and the Department of Economics. His current research examines the international migration of high-skilled labor, the causes of Mexican migration to the United States, the consequences of immigration on labor-market outcomes in the United States, the relationship between business cycles and global outsourcing, and international trade in motion pictures. His most recent book is *Why Does Immigration Divide America? Public Finance and Political Opposition to Open Borders* (Institute for International Economics, 2005). He is co-editor of the *Journal of Development Economics*, a research associate at the National Bureau of Economic Research, a member of the Council on Foreign Relations, and a senior research fellow at the Bureau for Research and Economic Analysis of Development. He obtained his BA in economics from Occidental College in 1986 and his Ph.D. in economics from MIT in 1992.

Gerald Jaynes

Gerald Jaynes is professor of economics and African American Studies, Yale University. Currently Director of Graduate Studies for African American Studies, he was Chair during 1990–1996. Jaynes was study director of the National Research Council's Committee on the Status of Black Americans and co-edited *A Common Destiny: Blacks and American Society*, National Academy Press, 1989. Jaynes' books also include *Branches Without Roots: Genesis of the Black Working Class in the American South*, Oxford, 1986 and *Immigration and Race: New Challenges for American Democracy*, Yale, 2000. Professor Jaynes has authored many articles on race relations and has testified to Congress on race and immigration. He holds a Ph.D. in economics from the University of Illinois.

Vernon M. Briggs, Jr.

Vernon M. Briggs Jr. is Emeritus Professor of Labor Economics at the New York State School of Labor and Industrial Relations at Cornell University. He also taught at the University of Texas at Austin for 14 years. Professor Briggs specializes in the area of human resource economics and public policy, and has also researched the subject of immigration policy and its effects on American workers. He has authored or co-authored numerous articles and books, including *Immigration Policy and the American Labor Force* (1984), *The Internationalization of the U.S. Economy: Its Labor Market Implications,* (1986), *Immigration and the U.S. Labor Market: Public Policy Gone Awry,* (1993), *Still an Open Door? U.S. Immigration Policy and the American Economy,* (1994), and *Mass Immigration and the National Interest: Policy Directions for the New Century,* 3rd Edition, (2003).

He was a member of the National Council on Employment Policy from 1977 to 1987 and Chairman of the Council from 1985–87. He has served on the Board of Directors of the

Corporation for Public and Private Ventures (1978–1984) and of the Center for Immigration Studies (1987 to present). He received his B.S. degree in economics from the University of Maryland and his M.A. and Ph.D. degrees in economics from Michigan State University.

Harry J. Holzer

Harry J. Holzer is a Professor of Public Policy at Georgetown University and a Senior Fellow at the Urban Institute in Washington DC. He is a former Chief Economist for the U.S. Department of Labor and a former Professor of Economics at Michigan State University. He is a Senior Affiliate of the National Poverty Center at the University of Michigan and a Research Affiliate of the Institute for Research on Poverty at the University of Wisconsin-Madison. He is also a Nonresident Senior Fellow with the Brookings Metropolitan Policy Program and a member of the editorial board at the *Journal of Policy Analysis and Management*. Holzer's research has focused primarily on the labor market problems of low-wage workers and other disadvantaged groups. His books include *The Black Youth Employment Crisis* (1986); *What Employers Want: Job Prospects for Less-Educated Workers* (1996); *Employers and Welfare Recipients: The Effects of Welfare Reform in the Workplace* (with Michael Stoll, 2001); *Moving Up or Moving On: Who Advances in the Low-Wage Labor Market* (with Fredrik Andersson and Julia Lane, 2005); *Reconnecting Disadvantaged Young Men* (with Peter Edelman and Paul Offner), Urban Institute Press, 2006; and *Reshaping the American Workforce in a Changing Economy* (co-edited with Demetra Nightingale), Urban Institute Press, 2007. He received his A.B. from Harvard in 1978 and his Ph.D. in Economics from Harvard in 1983.

Julie Hotchkiss

Julie Hotchkiss is a research economist and policy advisor in the regional group of the research department at the Federal Reserve Bank of Atlanta. Prior to joining the Bank in 2003, she was professor of economics at the Andrew Young School of Policy Studies at Georgia State University, where she still holds an adjunct position. Her major fields of study are earnings and employment differentials across different groups of workers, variations in employment and earnings across time, and policy implications of changes in labor supply. She is a member of the American Economic Association, the Southern Economic Association, the Western Economic Association, and the Society of Labor Economists. She serves on the Board of Trustees of the Southern Economic Association, on the Board the Committee of the Status of Women in the Economics Profession, and has served as co-editor for Southern Economic Journal and the Eastern Economic Journal. She received bachelor of arts degrees in economics and French from Willamette University. She earned her master's degree and doctorate in economics at Cornell University.

Steven A. Camarota

Steven A. Camarota is Director of Research at the Center for Immigration Studies in Washington, D.C. He is currently under contract with the Census Bureau as the lead researcher on a project examining the quality of immigrant data in the American Community Survey. His writing has been featured in the *Chicago Tribune, National Review, New York Times, Washington Post, USA Today, Public Interest,* and *Social Science Quarterly.* He has also appeared on radio and television news programs including *CNN*, *MSNBC*, *Fox News*, *NBC Nightly News*, and *ABC World News Tonight*, *CBS Evening News*, *National Public Radio*, and the PBS *NewsHour with Jim Lehrer*. His recent works with the Center for Immigration Studies include *Immigrants in the United States 2007: A Profile of the America's Foreign-born Population* and *100 Million More: Projecting the Impact of Immigration On the U.S. Population, 2007 to 2060*, *Illegitimate Nation: An Examination of Out-of-Wedlock Births Among Immigrants*, and *Natives The High Cost of Cheap Labor: Illegal Immigration and the Federal Budget*. He holds a Ph.D. from the University of Virginia in public policy analysis, and a Masters degree in political science from the University of Pennsylvania.

Richard Nadler

The late Richard Nadler served as president of the Americas Majority Foundation. His works with the Foundation included *Border Wars: The Impact of Immigration on the Latino Vote* and *Immigration and the Wealth of States*. Mr. Nadler previously served as researcher and writer for the National Advisory Commission on Adult Education in the U.S. Department of Education. He was a contributor to such publications as *National Review*, *Policy Review*, *The Wall Street Journal*, *Insight Magazine*, *Education Reform News*, and *Human Life Review*. Nadler founded the Missouri Taxpayers Watchdog Association, and served as its president from 1988–2000. He headed the 70/30 Committee (2000), the Republican Ideas Political Committee (2001), the Council for Better Government (2002), Americas Pac (2004), and Americas Majority (2005 through December, 2006.). In 2003, he served as political director of the Republican Leadership Coalition.

Carol M. Swain

Carol M. Swain is a professor of political science and law at Vanderbilt University. Before joining Vanderbilt in 1999, Professor Swain was a tenured associate professor of politics and public policy at Princeton University. Her books include *Black Faces, Black Interests: The Representation of African Americans in Congress*, *Debating Immigration* (ed.), *The New White Nationalism in America: Its Challenge to Integration*, and *Contemporary Voices of White Nationalism* (co-authored with Russ Nieli). She has appeared on numerous radio and television shows including C-Span's *Washington Journal*, PBS *NewsHour with Jim Lehrer*, *ABC World News Tonight*, *Fox News*, CNN's *Lou Dobbs Tonight*, CNN's *Anderson Cooper*, CNN's *Showbiz Tonight*, CNN's *Paula Zahn*, CNBC, *Tavis Smiley Show*, and National Public Radio's *Morning Edition*, *Here and Now*, and *The Connection*. She earned a bachelor's degree from Roanoke College, a master's degree from Virginia Polytechnic and State University, a Ph.D. from the University of North Carolina at Chapel Hill, and a master of studies in law from Yale University.

Commissioner Statements

Dissent Statement of Commissioners Michael Yaki and Arlan Melendez

We respectfully, but strongly, disagree with both the processes and outcomes involved with this Briefing Hearing and the instant Report. We believe that the Briefing Report and its findings and recommendations are merely the outcome of the most recent fatally flawed, inadequate process upon which the conservative majority of the Commission is reporting.

The Report's findings and recommendations are based upon a biased record. We believe that this underlying record was engineered in order to facilitate the narrow view which the recommendations embody. We are deeply concerned about the lack of balance on the panels which testified at the briefing which underlies this Report. Representatives from major, relevant non-governmental organizations were either not invited to testify or declined to do so due to mistrust of the motives of the Commission's conservative majority. As a result, issues affecting Hispanic and Latino Americans were discussed and debated without their participation or representation. This void in the record vitiates its validity, and, therefore, its usefulness.

Further, because the process which led to the majority's adoption of Part A was inappropriate, incomplete, and one-sided, it cannot serve as a basis from which valid findings can be distilled or meaningful recommendations drawn. Therefore, no useful weight can be accorded to the recommendations.

Concerns about immigration, falling wages and employment prospects for low-skilled workers require more than unbalanced panels and sketchy anecdotal testimony. The serious examination that any disparate impact study requires is completely missing from this report.

During challenging economic times, it is especially easy to target and scapegoat. What should be foremost in the minds of the Commission (but which are deeply hidden by the majority) are concerns regarding backlash and discrimination against communities because they are perceived as residing here illegally. Only in that full context can any meaningful report be produced. Alas, that is not and never has been the intent of the majority.

Statement and Rebuttal of Commissioner Gail Heriot

If the reader takes away one point from the Commission's report, it should be this: One of the consequences of the on-going illegal immigration of low-skilled workers into the United States is that it decreases the wages of low-skilled workers generally. This is simple supply and demand.

To be sure, the lowering of wages for low-skilled jobs is only one among many consequences of this immigration. There are others–good, bad and hard-to-classify. All of them must be taken into consideration in formulating sound immigration policy. Most, however, fall outside the jurisdiction of the Commission. The purpose of this briefing was to highlight a particular piece of the immigration puzzle–one that disproportionately affects American citizens and legal immigrants who are members of racial minorities.[103] It should not be confused with the puzzle as a whole.

It is also important not to overstate the case that illegal immigration depresses wages. Some critics of current immigration policy imagine that ending illegal immigration would result in American citizens and legal immigrants taking over all low-skilled jobs at higher wages. This is unlikely. In the medium- to long-term, some of these jobs would simply migrate to countries where labor is cheaper.[104] Others would be eliminated entirely. Homeowners, for example, may be willing to employ a gardener or housekeeper so long as wages remain very low. But if wages go up, they would do the work themselves.

Nevertheless, the fundamental point remains: There is a category of jobs that would remain in this country and pay higher wages in the absence of continued illegal immigration. No one should be surprised, therefore, to find that opposition to illegal immigration is very high among low-skilled workers, who bring home smaller paychecks on account of it. Similarly, no one should mistake for altruism the comparably greater support for illegal immigration among high-skilled workers, who sometimes personally benefit from low wages they pay to gardeners and housekeepers.[105]

Supporters of the status quo in immigration policy often accuse opponents of deep-seated. racism. One Senate staff member told Time Magazine, "There is a fear of white people being overrun by darker-skinned people."[106]   The truth is usually more mundane. Many of those who harbor strong feelings about illegal immigration–whether in support or in opposition–are motivated at least in part by ordinary self-interest, mostly, though by no means exclusively, of the economic variety.

The difficult job of Congress is to try to overcome the tendency to cater to one's own self interest and instead to determine what is in the interest of the nation as a whole.

---

[103] Several of our witnesses testified to the disproportionality point. See, e.g., Statement of Dr. Vernon Briggs at 38 ("Because most immigrants overwhelmingly seek work in the low skilled labor market and because the black American labor force is so disproportionately concentrated in this same low wage sector, there is little doubt that there is significant overlap in competition for jobs in this sector of the labor market"); Statement of Dr. Steven Camarota at 49 ("Black men are disproportionately employed at the bottom end of the labor market").

[104] In response to a question that I posed along these lines at our briefing, Dr. Harry Holzer testified that, because of the mobility of capital, increased enforcement of immigration laws would create an "enormous" disruptive effect. Transcript at 54. Dr. Gordon Hanson thought that such increased enforcement would also lead to capital outflows from the United States, but that such outflows would only partially offset the impact of increased enforcement on low-skilled wages. Transcript at 57.

[105] While illegal immigration is deeply unpopular with the general public, legal immigration is not. See, e.g. Alan Wolfe, One Nation After All (1998)(The division between legal and illegal immigrants "is one of the more tenaciously held distinctions in middle class America: the people with whom we spoke overwhelmingly support legal immigration and express disgust with the illegal variety").

[106] See Massimo Calabresi, "Is Racism Fueling the Immigration Debate?" Time (May 17, 2006).

As I understand it, the argument that competition from low-skilled, illegal immigrants has been a bad thing is more nuanced than the typical competition-is-hurting-us argument. Almost half a century after President Lyndon Johnson's war on poverty, we now have a significant number of citizens whose families have been unemployed for three and four generations. It's not just that they have never had a job themselves; frequently no one in their families has had a steady job. The skills necessary for employability that parents ordinarily pass on to their children–like punctuality, reliability, and the ability to get along with people outside one's family and circle of friends–often haven't been passed on.

Integrating third- and fourth-generation welfare recipients into the American mainstream is a tough job, although in recent years important steps have been taken to start the process. A higher demand for low-skilled labor would make the process easier. After decades of federal and state programs that only foster dependency, this is a step that could foster self-reliance and independence.

At the same time, welcoming immigrants is a strong tradition in this country. We are indeed a nation of immigrants and there can be no doubt that much of the nation's strength and vitality has come to us as a result of immigration.[107]

Perhaps the best I can add to this very complex debate is the observation that there should be a debate–a debate that considers all aspects of the issue, including the one featured in this briefing. With some luck, that debate will arrive at an immigration policy that a majority of us can support and that all of us can live with. A country that prides itself on the rule of law cannot afford to have one set of laws on paper and another in actual practice for long. Such a practice will ultimately corrode the rule of law.

Statement and Rebuttal of Commissioner Peter N. Kirsanow

In response to its alarming illegal immigration problem, Arizona recently enacted a statute that would allow state law enforcement officials to enforce federal immigration law. Ensuing controversy surrounding the law, and the reaction of various political actors to it, have once again thrust the issue of immigration reform to the forefront of the national debate. Beyond the rhetoric one fact seems clear—aside from encouraging disrespect for the rule of law, the lack of effective federal enforcement of the nation's borders[108] has produced significant

---

[107] Joel Millman has observed that immigrants are "our oldest and most dependable pool of 'riser,' a kind of demographic yeast that guarantees shared prosperity." Joel Millman, The Other Americans: How Immigrants Renew Our Country, Our Economy, and Our Values 314 (1997). Despite knowing little or no English upon their arrival, children from many immigrant groups often outperform native-born students on standardized tests. See Julian Lincoln Simon, The Economic Consequences of Immigration 99-100 (1999). Disproportionately high numbers of winners of the prestigious Westinghouse high school science competition have been born outside the United States. Id. See also Amanda Fairbanks, "New York Leads the Field in a High School Science Competition," The New York Times (January 31, 2008), available at http://www.nytimes.com/2008/01/31/nyregion/31contest html. Similarly, a disproportionately high percentage of American Nobel Prize winners have been immigrants.

[108] Dr. Vernon Briggs testified that lack of border management is not the only source of illegal immigration; some 40 percent of the nation's illegal immigrants are in the U.S. illegally as a result of overstaying their visas. U.S. Commission on Civil Rights, Briefing on the Impact of Illegal Immigration on the Wages and Employment Opportunities of Black Workers, Br. Tr. 52 (Apr. 4, 2008) (hereinafter "Impact of Illegal Immigration").

economic, political and social consequences for state and local governments and their associated communities.[109]   Yet to date, there has been little serious assessment or discussion of these impacts in crafting federal immigration proposals.   Furthermore, as the dissenting Commissioners' joint statement to this report demonstrates, hyperbole and mischaracterizations of opponents' positions too often substitute for responsible debate where the issue of illegal immigration is concerned.[110]

Addressing illegal immigration is difficult without first having a frank and honest debate about what we want our overall national immigration policy to accomplish.   As economist George Borjas observes in his book *Heaven's Door*, only by first defining our objectives can we answer the fundamental questions of how many immigrants to admit and who should be admitted.[111]   As Borjas notes, such questions cut to the heart of our "conception of what the United States is about."[112]   But building a political consensus regarding the purpose of immigration is no small task.   It is also one that is outside of this Commission's specific jurisdiction, which is why our briefing was designed to analyze only one of the many important issues in the immigration debate: the profound economic consequences for communities of color.

Does illegal immigration exert downward pressure on the wages and employment opportunities of low-skilled workers, particularly black workers, who tend to be represented in higher concentrations in the low- and unskilled workforce?   Our briefing revealed that there is general consensus among economists that it does (although that consensus breaks down over the magnitude of the effect and how or whether our national immigration policy should be modified as a result).   Yet this issue has not generated the kind of scrutiny by policymakers that its potentially serious consequences merit.[113]   In its limited treatment of the issue, much of the media has tended to downplay the impact of illegal immigration on low-skilled workers, tending to focus instead on the alleged overall benefits of the cheap labor provided by illegal immigrants to the U.S. economy.[114]   Perhaps a more searching analysis has been avoided because of the uncomfortable facts it might reveal, particularly to those for whom even the most speculative harm to minorities is often a trigger for robotic demagoguery.

---

[109] *See* Vernon Briggs, *The State of U.S. Immigration Policy: The Quandary of Economic Methodology and the Relevance of Economic Research to Know*, 5 GEO. MAS. L.R. 177, 181 (2009); Impact of Illegal Immigration Br. Tr. 114 (Testimony of Carol Swain).

[110] Joint Dissenting Statement of Commissioners Yaki and Melendez at page 71 of this report.   Commissioner Yaki's exchange with Dr. Vernon Briggs during the Commission's Apr. 4, 2008 briefing is similarly instructive. *See* Impact of Illegal Immigration Br. Tr. 66-77.

[111] GEORGE J. BORJAS, HEAVEN'S DOOR 5 (1999).

[112] *Id.*

[113] There have been some developments on this front recently, however: on January 26, 2010, Reps. Lamar Smith and Gary Miller announced the formation of the "Reclaim American Jobs Caucus" to focus on the impact of illegal immigration on the unemployment rate of U.S. workers, especially in light of the economic downturn. Gayle Cinquergrani, *Two GOP Lawmakers Form Caucus to Focus on Impact of Illegal Immigration on Jobs*, BNA DAILY LABOR REP., Jan. 28, 2010, at A-7.

[114] *See, e.g.* Chris Isidore, *Illegal workers: good for U.S. Economy*, CNNMONEY.COM (May 1, 2006).

Contrary to the dissenting Commissioners' assertion, the existence of a "majority" position regarding whether illegal immigration has some negative impact on the wages and job opportunities of black workers does not suggest that there is a majority position on the magnitude of that impact or on how heavily policymakers should weigh this impact in fashioning immigration reform proposals. Such positions necessarily go to individual Commissioners' weighing of the competing economic evidence and their perceptions of what the purpose of our national immigration policy should be. The Commission has taken no position on those points. There can be no other credible reading of our very limited and uncontroversial findings and sole recommendation, so it is difficult to determine the source of the dissenters' outrage.

Likewise, the dissenting Commissioners' contention that the record was biased by unbalanced panels is a plain misrepresentation of the facts. Particularly because the illegal immigration debate often tends to be so emotional and highly-charged, the briefing panels were designed to be research and data-focused. Our goal was to collect raw facts, without the self-serving interpretations often attached to them by partisans on both sides of the issue. The Office of the Staff Director contacted more than twenty-five different economists, academics and researchers who have worked on and contributed to scholarship on the questions at issue and who come from a variety of perspectives. In response to earlier staff requests for panelist recommendations, Commissioner Yaki provided names of three potential panelists with only two weeks to spare before the scheduled briefing, yet even on such short notice staff managed to secure the participation of one of his recommendations. Notably, Commissioner Yaki's list lacked the names of representatives from any advocacy organizations. Nonetheless, the minority decries the "fatally flawed" processes the Commission allegedly employs in preparing briefings, generating reports and making findings and recommendations. [115]

I write separately to highlight the available economic evidence pointing to the possibility that illegal immigration has a significant impact on the wages and employment opportunities of low-skilled workers, but also to note the limitations of the data, and to say that in certain respects, I would have gone further than my colleagues in the majority in making

---

[115] To the dissenting Commissioners' suggestion that "representatives from major, relevant non-governmental organizations" declined to participate in the briefing "due to their mistrust of the motives of the Commission's conservative majority," I will only note that on at least two recent occasions, briefing witnesses who might share the minority Commissioners' views, have accepted staff invitations to participate as briefing panelists only to pull back from participating late in the planning process. The circumstances surrounding these often last-minute withdrawals are, at the very least, curious. *See, e.g.,* U.S. Commission on Civil Rights, Briefing on Specifying English as the Common Language of the Workplace (Dec. 12, 2008) (in which two panelists expected to present views opposed to specifying English as the language of the workplace, cancelled the night before and morning of the briefing, one invoking the minority's "panel balance concerns" refrain (while ensuring at the same time the very problem which she alleged)); *see also* U.S. Commission on Civil Rights, Briefing on Encouraging Minority Students To Pursue Careers In Science, Technology, Engineering And Math (STEM) (Sept. 12, 2008) (in which former Secretary of Energy Hazel O'Leary, President of historically black Fisk University, cancelled her scheduled appearance only days before the Commission's briefing. During the hearing, Commissioner Yaki expressed approval for her cancellation, stating, "I know that former Secretary O'Leary cancelled from the HBCU, but I am actually kind of glad she did . . ," right after lamenting the alleged lack of balance on the briefing panel). STEM Br. Tr. 146.

recommendations, particularly as they relate to the tenor of the debate over illegal immigration.

In the ensuing period between our briefing and the issuance of this report, the precarious economic position of low-skilled workers—and of black workers in particular—has been demonstrated once again. The nation has experienced what some have termed a "Great Recession." But "the pain of this labor market downturn has not been widely shared across age, educational or occupational groups,"[116] with young workers (ages 16-24), non-college educated male adults, blue collar workers and black males bearing the brunt of the nation's economic woes.[117]

According to the Bureau of Labor Statistics, in April 2010 joblessness for blacks hit 16.5 percent, compared with 9.0 percent for whites and 12.5 percent for Hispanics. The Washington Post reports that in October 2009 joblessness for young black men aged 16-24 hit Great Depression proportions of 34.5 percent, "more than three times the rate for the general U.S. population."[118] Since members of this age group are relatively new to the job market, dislocation caused by the lack or loss of crucial gateway job experiences can have damaging future consequences, including wholesale labor force withdrawal.

Considering the unemployment rates of low-skilled workers generally, those with less than a high school diploma had an unemployment rate of 14.7 percent in April 2010. For those with a high school diploma but no college, the unemployment rate was 10.6 percent. But for those with a bachelor's degree it was 4.6 percent—within the range of what labor economists deem an "acceptable" level of structural unemployment or "full employment." Unemployment rates have been higher in industries that employ a high number of illegal immigrant workers. These rates do not account for the growing percentage of low-skill American workers leaving the labor market altogether.[119]

---

[116] ANDREW SUM ET AL., THE DEEP DEPRESSION IN BLUE COLLAR LABOR MARKETS IN THE U.S.: THEIR IMPLICATIONS FOR FUTURE ECONOMIC STIMULUS AND WORKFORCE DEVELOPMENT POLICIES, (Dec. 2009), *available at* http://www.massworkforce.com/documents/NationalBlueCollarWorkersReport.pdf.

[117] *Id.* at 1. *See also* Eric Eckholm, *Working Poor and Young Hard Hit By Economic Downturn*, N.Y. TIMES (Nov. 8, 2008), at A26, *available at* http://www.nytimes.com/2008/11/09/us/09young html; Andrew M. Sum and Paul E. Harrington, *Two Kinds of Immigration*, BOS. GLOBE (Oct. 16, 2006), *available at* http://www.boston.com/news/globe/editorial_opinion/oped/articles/2006/10/16/two_kinds_of_immigration/ ("Available evidence shows that there has been a high rate of displacement of younger, native-born male workers and younger women without four-year college degrees by newer immigrants, especially undocumented immigrants.").

[118] *See* BUREAU OF LABOR STATISTICS UNEMPLOYMENT DATA (Apr. 2010). *See also* V. Dion Haynes, *Blacks Hit Hard by Economy's Punch*, WASH. POST (Nov. 24, 2009), available at http://www.washingtonpost.com/wp-dyn/content/article/2009/11/23/AR2009112304092 html.

[119] According to researchers, one possible response to immigration by native workers is wholesale labor force withdrawal.

> Labor force withdrawal is important in its own right since it directly reflects an economic loss and it weakens the attachment of low-wage native workers to the labor market. But it is also important because it affects the measurement of the economic consequences of immigration. When native workers respond to immigration by dropping out of the labor force, they reduce its measured impact for two reasons. First, dropouts are subtracted out from both the numerator and the denominator of the unemployment rate. Second, the workers who withdraw are the lowest-wage

Incidents of underemployment are also highest among high school dropouts and graduates with no post-secondary schooling, affecting blacks and Hispanics most heavily.[120] Finally, unemployment has persisted for longer stretches during the latest recession—a mean of 29 weeks at the end of 2009—with a majority of the unemployed leaving the labor market permanently.[121] Again, workers with the least educational attainment, a disproportionate share of whom are black males, suffered most.

Indeed, the labor market position of low-skill workers has been steadily eroding over the past few decades.[122] For example, the period between 1980 and 2000 saw a dramatic increase in the wage gap between high school dropouts and more educated workers.[123] With respect to the economic prospects of black low-skill workers specifically, one panelist testified that the employment rate of black high school dropouts fell by 30 percentage points over a slightly longer period—between 1960 to 2000 (from 72 percent to 42 percent).[124] Male high school graduates fared little better, and at both educational levels the situation was dire for white males but markedly worse for blacks.[125]

Changing labor market conditions, including a steady reduction in overall low-skill jobs in the United States, overseas competition from globalization and increased modernization of industry have all had an impact on the job prospects of low-skill workers. These developments also coincided with a dramatic rise in the number of immigrants—legal and

---

native workers who most directly compete with immigrants. Consequently, the average wage of the native workers who remain in the labor force is increased by sample selection effects.
Hannes Johannsson and Steven Shulman, *Immigration and the Employment of African American Workers*, DEBATING IMMIGRATION 79, 78 (Carol M. Swain, ed., 2007).

[120] ANDREW SUM ET AL., LABOR UNDERUTILIZATION PROBLEMS OF U.S. WORKERS ACROSS HOUSEHOLD INCOME GROUPS AT THE END OF THE GREAT RECESSION: A TRULY GREAT DEPRESSION AMONG THE NATION'S LOW INCOME WORKERS AMIDST FULL EMPLOYMENT AMONG THE MOST AFFLUENT 3, n.4 (Feb. 2010), *available at* http://www.clms neu.edu/publication/documents/Labor_Underutilization_Problems_of_U.pdf (Report Prepared for the C.S. Mott Foundation). The authors note that "underemployment contributes in an important way to the high and rising degree of income inequality in the United Sates and to growing poverty in the recession." *Id.* at 4.

[121] *Id.* at 7.

[122] Several of the briefing panelists acknowledged, and the Commission found, that the average worker with a high school degree or less earns less today, adjusted for inflation, than someone with a similar education earned thirty-five years ago. Impact of Illegal Immigration Br. Tr. 49 (Camarota Statement); Impact of Illegal Immigration Br. Tr. 25 (Hanson Statement); Impact of Illegal Immigration Br. Tr. 29-30 (Jaynes Statement). Dr. Briggs testified that the low-skilled labor market is most vulnerable to economic hardship, which has been borne out by recent events. Impact of Illegal Immigration Br. Tr. 26.

[123] BORJAS, *supra* note 4, at 63.

[124] Impact of Illegal Immigration Br. Tr. 25 (Hanson Testimony),. *See also*, U.S. COMMISSION ON CIVIL RIGHTS, IMPACT OF ILLEGAL IMMIGRATION ON THE WAGES AND EMPLOYMENT OPPORTUNITIES OF BLACK WORKERS BRIEFING REPORT (CITE TO ACTUAL TITLE OF REPORT)29-30 (DATE) (Jaynes Submitted Testimony).

[125] IMPACT OF ILLEGAL IMMIGRATION BR. REP. 30 (Jaynes Submitted Testimony) ("Thus, although in 1970, black high school graduates and college graduates ages 25-34 had similar employment rates (90 percent versus 90.4 percent), by 1985 high school graduates had an employment rate 13 percentage point s lower (66.3 percent versus 79.6 percent). The employment rate of same age black high school dropouts during 1985 was 57.2 percent, more than 20 points lower than the college graduates."). *Id.*

illegal—entering the United States yearly since 1965. The Bureau of National Affairs reports that between 2000 and 2008 the U.S. foreign-born population grew to 22.1 percent, nearly four times faster than the 6.3 percent growth of the native-born population, according a Pew Hispanic Center Survey released earlier this year.[126] As of 2008, over 16 percent of the nation's full-time civilian labor force was composed of foreign-born workers. In fact, foreign-born labor accounted for nearly 50 percent of the overall growth in the labor force between 2000 and 2006.[127] It is estimated that nearly 30 percent of the total foreign-born workforce consists of illegal immigrants (7.1 million of the estimated 12 million illegal immigrants in the United States).

Of course, an increase in the foreign-born population, standing alone, reveals little, if anything, about illegal immigration's role in overall worker dislocation, let alone black unemployment rates. Somewhat more telling is information regarding foreign-born workers' educational attainment and skill levels relative to the native-born population,[128] the occupations and industries in which such workers tend to concentrate, and well-known impediments to black labor force participation. These data raise serious questions for a society coping with alarming unemployment rates among low and unskilled blacks.

Consider, for example, the following:

- *Blacks are represented in high concentrations in the low-skill labor market.* One third of the entire black labor force is made up of low-skilled workers, and blacks comprise 10 percent of the 50 million low-skilled adults in the civilian labor force in the United States.[129] Six in 10 black adult males have a high school degree or less, compared with four out of 10 for whites.

- *Recent immigrants tend to be low-skilled; this is especially true of illegal immigrants.* Data show that over the last 50 years, there has been a precipitous decline in the relative educational attainment of immigrants.[130] For example, according to 2007 census data, of those immigrants entering the U.S. (both legally and illegally) between 2000 and 2007, only 24.6 percent had a high school education; 35.5 percent had not completed high school. This compares with 30.9 percent and 7.5 percent, for

---

[126] Larry Swisher, *U.S. Foreign Born Population Increased 22.1 Percent During 2000-2008, Pew Says*, BNA DAILY REP., Jan. 25, 2010, at A-8.

[127] Briggs, *supra* note 2, at 178.

[128] Both Borjas and Briggs note the significance of foreign-born workers' human capital endowments relative to native-born workers in determining the social and economic consequences of immigration. Borjas, *supra* note 4 at 19; *Impact of Immigration on Recent Immigrants and Black and Hispanic Citizens: Hearing Before the Subcomm. On Immigration and Claims of the H. Comm. on the Judiciary*, 106th Cong. 69-75 (Mar. 11, 1999) (Testimony of Vernon M. Briggs).

[129] Impact of Illegal Immigration Br. Rep. at 37 (Briggs Submitted Testimony).

[130] BORJAS, *supra* note 4, at 21-22 (Borjas reports that in 1960, 66 percent of immigrant men were high school dropouts compared with 53 percent of native-born men, but immigrants actually earned about 4 percent more than natives. But by the late 1990s, immigrants were far more likely than native workers to be high school dropouts (34 percent compared to only 9 percent for natives). What had previously been an earnings advantage for foreign-born workers now became a tremendous disadvantage, with immigrants earning about 23 percent less than natives by 1998).

native-born American workers, respectively. Such workers are thus more likely to be concentrated in the low-skill labor market.

- *Native-born low-skill workers appear to be dropping out of the labor market, while rates of immigrants have increased.* A 2006 Center for Immigration Studies analysis showed that the percentage of native-born Americans in the labor force with either a high school diploma or less fell from 59 percent to 56 percent in the preceding five years.[131] The study estimated that approximately 1.5 million native-born Americans with a high school diploma or less left the workforce during that period. During the same period, the number of immigrants in the workforce (legal and illegal) with high school diplomas or less *increased* by almost the same amount—1.6 million.

- *Low-skilled immigrants and blacks are concentrated in the same occupations and specific segments of the labor market, suggesting they compete for work.* The same CIS study referenced above reveals that the occupations with the highest percentage of illegal immigrants are occupations that also have the highest unemployment rates for the native born. These same occupations happen to be among those that have traditionally employed the highest percentage of black workers, e.g., building cleaning and maintenance,[132] food preparation[133] and construction.

Thus, while illegal immigration alone cannot be said to have caused negative employment outcomes for black workers, there is ample evidence to suggest that at a minimum, it has had an aggravating effect on both the displacement of low-skilled American workers and the racial divide in employment. This is because illegal immigration tends to increase the supply of low-skilled, low-wage labor already available in the U.S. labor market. Geographic

---

[131] Steven Camarota, *Dropping Out: Immigrant Entry and Native Exit from the Labor Market, 2000-2005*, CIS BACKGROUNDER (Mar. 2006*), available at* http://www.cis.org/articles/2006/back206.pdf. For a discussion of how the "dropping out" phenomenon impacts reporting of unemployment numbers, *see also* discussion in Johannsson and Shulman, *supra* note 13.

[132] A 1988 Government Accountability Office (GAO) study of Los Angeles janitorial services found that when several small firms began hiring illegal immigrants as janitors for lower pay, building owners dropped contracts with the companies that employed black workers in favor of the cheaper contractor. As the immigrant-employing firms overtook a larger share of the market, local janitorial industry wages dropped by over a dollar—from a peak of $6.58 an hour in 1983 to $5.63 an hour in 1985. The number of black janitors in L.A. also dropped from about 2,500 in the late 1970s to only 600 by 1985. GOV'T ACCOUNTABILITY OFFICE, GAO/PEMD-99-13BR, ILLEGAL ALIENS: INFLUENCE OF ILLEGAL WORKERS ON WAGES AND WORKING CONDITIONS OF LEGAL WORKERS, (Mar. 1988).

[133] Industry-specific impacts of an influx of illegal immigrant labor are instructive. For a discussion of the decline of wages, employment opportunities and conditions in the meatpacking/poultry industries, as well as evidence that strict enforcement produces more job opportunities for native-born, displaced workers at higher wages, *see* Evan Perez and Corey Dale, *An immigration raid aids blacks for a time*, WSJ (Jan. 17, 2007), *available at* http://www.post-gazette.com/pg/07017/754517-28.stm; Joel Dyer, *Meatpacking industry has a long history of reliance on immigrant laborer*, FT. COLLINS WKLY. (Dec. 26, 2006), *available at* http://www.greeleytribune.com/article/20061226/NEWS/112230087; Bill Jackson, *More applicants applying for Swift & Co.*, THE TRIBUNE (Dec. 20, 2006), *available at* http://www.greeleytribune.com/article/20061220/BUSINESS/112200084; (MEGAHAN MURPHY IS NOT LISTED AS AUTHOR ON THIS SITE) *Former Dallas employees sue Swift alleging wage manipulation*, ASSOCIATED PRESS (Dec. 18, 2006), *available at* http://www.thedenverchannel.com/news/10561323/detail.html.

proximity (i.e. concentration in large urban centers of both blacks and immigrants), and illegal immigrants' low human capital endowments bring them in direct labor competition with native-born (as well as legal immigrant) low-skill workers, especially blacks and new, legal immigrants, who are more heavily concentrated in unskilled occupations. Moreover, wage data shows that this increase has occurred in the absence of any shortage of available unskilled labor in the U.S.[134] A large share of less-educated native born workers are employed in what are considered high-immigrant occupations; even in such occupations, the majority of workers are still natives.[135] These facts tend to belie the notion that there are jobs Americans just won't do. The job market is simply not segmented into "exclusively immigrant" or "exclusively native jobs," regardless of where one is in the labor market.[136] It is true that the current recession has hit immigrant workers (both legal and illegal) the hardest in terms of unemployment numbers, but the least educated immigrants (and thereby the least skilled) still have a lower unemployment rate than their native-born counterparts.[137]

According to National Assessment of Educational Progress statistics, the average black high school graduate continues to lag years behind his white counterparts in academic proficiency. Low educational attainment signals that a significant percentage of black workers are likely to be low or unskilled, where they will be competing against illegal immigrants—a cohort motivated by the fact that the U.S. minimum wage is 10 times higher than what they would earn in their native countries—for the same low-skilled jobs. These dismal education figures, combined with the significant impediments that flow from fragile family structures and a 70 percent out-of-wedlock birth rate, portend more deleterious long term implications for blacks than for other groups. Surely, more serious study is necessary in the run-up to any immigration reform proposals that may aggravate both the displacement of low-skilled American workers and the racial divide in employment.

For those of us who value the contributions of immigrants but who maintain that the nation should adopt an immigration policy that does not increase the social and economic inequities that already exist in the United States, pointing out that the plight of the nation's most vulnerable workers (and of blacks as a subset of those) must be a consideration in any immigration reform proposals hardly seems like a controversial proposition. Policymakers would be negligent if they ignored the social and economic implications of increasing the nation's low-skilled labor supply. Stemming the tide of illegal immigration alone will not alone improve the outcomes for legal low-skilled workers, but as my colleague Gail Heriot notes, it is definitely a piece of the puzzle.

Furthermore, one of the challenges of the debate is honesty regarding what the data show and what they do not show. This is complicated by methodology and data limitations, which either cannot or do not assess immigration policy's effects in the same way or meaningfully

---

[134] PATRICK MCHUGH, CENTER FOR IMMIGRATION STUDIES, TRENDS IN IMMIGRANT AND NATIVE UNEMPLOYMENT 2 (May 2009) ("There is little evidence of a labor shortage, particularly for less-educated workers. In the first quarter of 2009 there are almost 31 million natives and immigrants with a high school degree or less unemployed or not in the labor force," i.e. neither working nor looking for work.).

[135] Camarota, *supra* note 24, at 15.

[136] *Id.*

[137] *Id.* at 1.

distinguish between different categories of immigrants by how they were admitted. I agree with Dr. Briggs that under these circumstances, it is difficult for policymakers to design remedies that best promote the national interest rather than the policy preferences of special interest groups. I further concur with his recommendation that as a result, "a more nuanced methodology that encourages an understanding of historical experiences, an awareness of changing domestic economic conditions, and an appreciation of the evolutionary development of the component policies that comprise immigration policy would be a preferred option."[138]

Given these circumstances, participants in the debate over immigration should take greater care not to overstate or misrepresent the conclusions that can be drawn from the currently available data. At the same time, those who express concern regarding the impact of *illegal* immigration cannot be dismissed or demonized as being "anti-immigrant." Intemperate language and accusations of nativism and racism only further confound the debate. Politicians on both sides of the aisle should care enough about immigration policy and its ramifications for the national interest to speak honestly, avoiding the inflammatory words that have caused the discussions regarding illegal immigration to devolve.

Rebuttal of Commissioners Michael Yaki and Arlan Melendez

The plain truth that the majority refuses to acknowledge is that the record is considerably mixed on whether illegal immigrants create any measurable or significant impact upon the wages and employment opportunities of African-Americans. There is even considerable debate whether, for the group of low-skilled, low-educated Americans, competition with undocumented workers creates the displacement effects that the majority seems to consider a fait accompli.[139] Labor economist and University of California at Berkeley Professor David Card has been a leading proponent of the theory that illegal immigration does not have the significant adverse employment and wage effects on low-skilled, native-born workers that are commonly presumed.[140] In fact, Card reasons, the presence of low-skilled immigrants may indeed have benefits for such Americans. On this overarching point, Card states that:

> More than two decades of research on the local labor market impacts of immigration has reached a near consensus that increased immigration has a small but discernible negative effect on the *relative* wages of low-skilled native workers (i.e., the ratio of low-skilled wages to wages in the middle of the skill distribution). Less is known

---

[138] Briggs, *supra* note 2, at 192.

[139] And it must be noted – as if it wasn't patently obvious – that the category of "low-skilled" or "low-educated" or "high school drop-out" is not, in and of itself, a racial, ethnic, religious, or gender classification that is within the jurisdiction of the Commission on Civil Rights.

[140] Other researchers have also found that the impact of immigrants upon the wages of native-born workers is minimal at most. For other recent examinations of the economic effects of immigration on native-born racial minorities and/or low-skilled workers, see George Borjas, Jeffery Grogger & Gordon H. Hanson, *Immigration and African American Employment Opportunities: The Response of Wages, Employment, and Incarceration to Labor Supply Shocks* (NBER Working Paper 12518, 2006); Deborah Reed and Sheldon Danziger, *The Effects of Recent Immigration on Racial/Ethnic Labor Market Differences*, AMERICAN ECONOMIC REVIEW 97, No. 2 (2007); Gordon H. Hanson, *The Economics and Policy of Illegal Immigration in the United States* (Migration Policy Institute 2009).

about the impact on the average level of native wages, but theoretical reasoning, as well as the evidence presented here (and in a few other studies, mainly at the national level) suggests a small positive effect . . . . Taken together with the labor market evidence, it seems that the direct economic impacts of immigration on existing native residents of major U.S. cities are relatively small, and may well be positive.[141]

Professor Card's own years of research and findings support the conclusions of others which show that any impact of immigration upon the average wages of native low-skilled workers is "relatively modest."[142] Specifically, his analysis indicates that in American cities with high numbers of low-skilled immigrants, "the relative wages of [native] workers in the lowest skill group are about 3-4 percent lower [than in low-immigrant cities]...."[143] Card further concludes that actual average wages for native, low-skilled workers may actually rise as much as 10 percent in cities such as Los Angeles with high immigrant numbers. Obviously, he says, "this effect is more than large enough to offset the 4-5 percent reduction in the <u>relative</u> wages of low-skilled [native] workers."[144] Therefore, "even though the <u>relative</u> wages of low-skilled natives are depressed in high-immigrant cities, the absolute <u>level</u> of their wages appears to be higher" than in low-immigrant cities.[145] It appears, then, that the majority's worries are the proverbial much ado about nothing.

Card's work regarding the impact of immigration on low-skilled native workers is largely, but not universally, accepted within his field.[146] Fellow economists George Borjas and Lawrence Katz of Harvard University opined in 2005 that immigration between 1980 and 2000 resulted in a wage decline for native-born high school drop-outs by 8.2 percent.[147] Given that high-school dropouts are presumed to be low-skilled workers, this figure indicates approximately double the impact that Card ascertained. But even if Borjas and Katz were accurate, Card still finds the effect of their number to be minimal. "That's 40 cents an hour (less) as a result of 20 years of Mexican immigration. In the several studies I've done over almost 20 years, if there are such effects (lowering of wages), they are very, very small."[148]

However, Lawrence Katz himself has minimized the conflict between the percentages (and related impacts) that he and Borjas published and that of Card. Katz has "acknowledged [that] the original analysis used some statistically flimsy data," and that the result should

---

[141] David Card, "How Immigration Effects U.S. Cities" June 2007, http://www.irle.berkeley.edu/events/fall07/symposium/card.pdf at p. 32. Retrieved May 24, 2010. (emphasis in original).

[142] *Id.*, p. 18

[143] *Id.*

[144] *Id.*, p. 20 (emphasis in original).

[145] *Id.* (emphasis in original).

[146] Cowen, Tyler, and Rothschild, Daniel M., "Each Is Good For the Other," Ft. Worth Star Telegram (TX), May 17, 2006, p. B-15.

[147] Borjas, George and Katz, Lawrence, "The Evolution of the Mexican-Born Workforce in the United States," NBER Working Paper # 11281, National Bureau of Economic Research, Cambridge, MA, April 2005 at p. 37.

[148] Said, Carolyn, "The Immigration Debate: Effect on Economy Depends on Viewpoint," San Francisco Chronicle (CA), May 21, 2006, p. A-13.

have been 3.6 percent rather than 8.2 percent.[149] Further, "Katz says people are putting too much emphasis on this analysis and the 8 percent figure in particular. 'This was a back-of-the-envelope simulation at the end of the papers,' [according to Katz]."[150] With Katz's revision of his figures to be in line with Card's, the challenge to Card is substantively eviscerated.[151] [152]

The Card analysis, as has been noted, received little to no attention by the majority either in the preparation of the hearing or this report, despite its abundant acceptance and citations by scholars and the media.[153] The majority's omission of significant, highly respected scholarly work which is directly on point certainly calls the majority's objectivity and agenda into question.

Scapegoating is the tried and true method of dealing with all new immigrant populations, legal or illegal. The fact is that the true civil rights issue that is raised by anti-illegal immigrant discourse, such as that published by the majority, is discrimination against those native groups that bear the characteristics of the population targeted for enforcement – in other words, racial profiling of Americans.[154] But that is not, apparently, a concern for the majority.

---

[149] Porter, Eduardo, "Lowest U.S. Wages Have Fallen But Illegals Aren't Solely to Blame," Denver Rocky 'Mountain News (CO), April 22, 2006, p. 2C.

[150] Pender, Kathleen, "Labor's Complex Situation," San Francisco Chronicle (CA), April 26, 2006, p. C-1.

[151] Borjas has also been involved in research that found a minimal impact on low-skilled native workers similar to what Card has determined. Borjas served on the Committee on Population of the National Research Council's Commission on Behavioral and Social Sciences and Education. This group issued a 1997 report, "The New Americans: Economics, Demographics, and Fiscal Effects of Immigration," Borjas' committee found that "[T]he wages of these [low-skill] native-born Americans may have fallen some 5 percent over the past 15 years. Yet even in local labor markets with high numbers of new immigrants, overall job opportunities and wages for the native-born are not significantly affected by immigration. The effects may be minor because natives who compete directly with immigrants may be moving to other areas, and because immigration brings overall benefits to most Americans." Galvin, Molly, "Overall U.S. Economy Gains From Immigration, But It's Costly to Some States and Localities," News From the Academies, May 17, 1997, retrieved May 24, 2010 from http://www8 nationalacademies.org/onpinews/newsitem.aspx?RecordID=5779.

[152] It is interesting to note that both Card and Borjas are immigrants to the United States. David Card was born in Canada and George Borjas was born in Cuba. Cowen and Rothschild, *supra*.

[153] On the Fence: Are Illegal Immigrants Good or Bad for the U.S. Economy, http://knowledge.wharton.upenn.edu/article.cfm?articleid=175. Retrieved May 24, 2010; Will Illegal Immigration Offset a Wage Hike? MSNBC, Jan. 10, 2007, http://www.msnbc.msn.com/id/16541091. Retrieved May 24, 2010. See also "Cost of Illegal Immigration May Be Less Than Meets The Eye," New York Times, April 16, 2006, http://www nytimes.com/2006/04/16/business/yourmoney/16view.html. Retrieved May 24, 2010; Q&A: Illegal Immigrants and the Economy, NPR, March 30, 2006, http://www npr.org/templates/story/story.php?storyId=5312900. Retrieved May 24, 2010.

[154] The most obvious, and immediate, example is the law recently enacted by Arizona empowering law enforcement officers to stop people who they have a "reasonable suspicion" of being undocumented persons. See, e.g., Michael Yaki, "Why the Arizona Law is Anti-Immigrant, not Anti-Illegal Immigration" http://www.sfgate.com/cgi-bin/blogs/yaki/detail?entry_id=6219. Retrieved May 24, 2010, and Michael Yaki, "Arizona Anti-Immigrant Law: How A Law That Is "Neutral" Can Be Racist," http://www.sfgate.com/cgi-bin/blogs/yaki/detail?entry_id=6243. Retrieved May 24, 2010.

Commissioner Heriot asserts that if the readers of this briefing report only take away one point from it that point should be: "One of the consequences of the on-going illegal immigration of low-skilled workers into the United States is that it decreases the wages of low-skilled workers generally. This is simple supply and demand."[155] The real world economic effect of immigration, legal and illegal, on low-skilled workers, however, is not something that can be so easily simplified. The demand for labor is not static or inelastic such that an increase in the supply of labor would necessarily depress wages. Rather, both the demand and the supply of labor are dynamic, and as such, the effect that immigration has and has had on both has been either difficult to ascertain or miniscule.[156]

Professor Card's results from his long-term work are in direct conflict with Commissioner Heriot's generalized assertion. To the contrary, as discussed above, Card finds that, in American cities with high numbers of low-skilled immigrants, native-born low-skilled workers appear to have only a 3 to 4 percent loss in relative wages and an increase in actual wages.[157]

Further, Card notes that the labor supply which the low-skill immigrant pool provides may actually be helping some sectors of the American economy grow. When an area has a large influx of immigrants, Card finds that "[t]he labor market can adjust. It can increase in areas where there are a lot of unskilled immigrants. Employers can move in who can support that."[158] By way of example, Card has stated that:

> 20 years ago when I first moved to the U.S., only very rich people had their lawns cut by someone else. The cost of hiring someone to do that got so low because of the supply of landscapers and firms that specialized in hiring immigrants, it created a sector of the economy that ... wasn't counted as part of GDP [Gross Domestic Product] before.[159]

Growth in the home health care industry has also been fueled by immigrants willing to work as home health aides. As Card said, "If those (immigrants) weren't here, most people would have their mothers and grandmothers living with them. When that kind of labor is available, people will think of how to exploit it."[160]

In line with Card's expectation, the American economy is believed to be absorbing large numbers of illegal immigrants in an array of industries. Findings indicate that

> [i]llegal immigrants make up nearly 5 percent of the U.S. workforce, with large numbers of them in certain industries that require few skills and little education,

---

[155] Commissioner Heriot's Concurrence, published herewith.

[156] The dynamic nature of the labor market, and the extremely limited effects that immigration has upon it, have been amply demonstrated by those cited in footnote 2, *supra*.

[157] Card at pp. 18, 20.

[158] Said, *supra*.

[159] *Id.*

[160] *Id.*

according to the Pew Hispanic Center. They make up about 14 percent of construction workers, 17 percent of cleaning crews and 12 percent of food-preparation workers. One in 4 farmhands in America is an illegal immigrant.[161]

Professor Card's two-plus decades of work on the issues, the minimal impact he finds upon the low-skilled native worker pool, the complexities and nuances of the questions, and the large number of illegal immigrants being employed across industries all, we believe, counsel against acceptance of Commissioner Heriot's one-dimensional assertion.

Commissioner Heriot's concurrence admits that, "the purpose of this briefing was to highlight"[162] the depression of wages and employment that the conservative majority had presumed was the effect of immigration, and which they presumed "disproportionately affects American citizens and legal immigrants who are members of racial minorities."[163] This admission only further supports our contention that these purported negative effects were seemingly a foregone conclusion for a majority of the Commission. As we have noted before, the majority's obvious and strong presuppositions seemingly made it impossible for the Commission to recruit representatives from the immigrant advocacy community for participation in, and testimony during, our briefing.[164]

In addition to our substantive disagreements with body of the majority's report, we have a procedural concern as well. The manner in which the Findings and Recommendations section of this Briefing Report was adopted only further supports our understanding that this whole endeavor was one-sided and incomplete. The findings and recommendations were approved at the February 26, 2010 meeting of the Commission. The findings and recommendations that were adopted were substitutions proposed by several Commissioners for the findings and recommendations prepared by the staff.

We of course have no categorical objections to Commissioners drafting and proposing amendments or substitutions; rather, such input is an important part of the Commission's internal dialogue. However, in this case, the text of the Commissioner-authored findings and recommendations were not shared with all Commissioners prior to the meeting and vote.[165] Additional amendments to these substitute amendments were made verbally during the meeting. The result of these sloppy procedures was that no Commissioner at the meeting could actually repeat the text of what was being voted on—not even the authors of the amendments themselves![166] Under such circumstances, we find it impossible to think that

---

[161] McGee, Patrick, "Do Immigrants Take Jobs From U.S. Workers?," Fort Worth Star-Telegram (TX), August 11, 2006, p. A-1.

[162] Heriot, *supra*

[163] *Id.*

[164] *See* Briefing Transcript, pp. 65-67 (Commissioner Yaki speaking). *See, also*, USCCR Briefing Transcript, Dec. 12, 2008, pp. 9-10 (Commissioner Yaki speaking).

[165] Since the February 26 meeting was a telephonic meeting, it was also not even possible to belatedly share hard copies of the text of the amendments—although we would have also objected to the failure to provide adequate time for Commissioners to consider the substantial revisions to the text.

[166] *See* USCCR Meeting Transcript, Feb. 26, 2010, pp. 28, 44.

the adoption of these findings and recommendations was done in a deliberative manner, and believe that the public should view them—and rest of this report—with great skepticism.